CW00556940

The Story of
JAYWICK SANDS ESTATE

An aerial view of Jaywick.

The Story of
JAYWICK SANDS ESTATE

Mary Lyons

Phillimore

1996
Reprinted in paperback 2005

Published by
PHILLIMORE & CO. LTD
Shopwyke Manor Barn, Chichester, West Sussex, England

© Mary Lyons, 1996, 2005

ISBN 1 86077 336 2

Printed and bound in Great Britain by
BIDDLES LTD
www.biddles.co.uk

Contents

List of Illustrations

Frontispiece: An aerial view of Jaywick

Acknowledgements

No-one can ever write a local history without reference to those that have gone before. In particular I have leant heavily on the works of Mr. I. Banks, Mr. N. Jacobs, Mr. G. Hardwick, Mr. D. Hardy, Mr. K. Palmer, Mr. K. Walker and Mr. C. Ward. It is inevitable that on occasion certain of their ideas will appear in paraphrased form. Any errors, however, are of course my own.

The illustrations appear by kind permission of the following: Clacton Historical Society, 35, 96; Mr. B. Davies, 99-101; East Anglian Times, 93; East Essex Gazette, 61, 86, 98; Essex Police, 81; Essex Records Office, 5, 6, 9, 11-13, 17-20, 22, 23, 25-27, 31-33, 39, 40, 42-45, 49, 50, 55, 56, 62, 66-71, 74, 76, 77, 82, 95; Mr. B. Fenn, 85; Mr. C. Hart, 64, 102; W.J. Nicholls, 75; D. Patel, 103; Phillimore & Co. Ltd., 2; Eileen Phillips, 105, 106; Glenda Selwood, 57, 72, 73, 83, 91; Mr. S. Smith, 79, 80, 87; Stedman Collection, Clacton Library, 1, 3, 7, 8, 21, 28, 29, 41, 46, 48, 52, 58, 63; Stedman brochure, 4, 10, 14-16, 24, 30, 34, 36-38, 47, 51, 54, 65, 90, 108; Mr. N. Stedman, 59; Mrs. H. Wright, 84. The remainder are from the author's own collection.

My thanks must also go to Mrs. J. Holly, Mrs. Giles, Mr. C. Hart, Mr. W. Nicholson, Mrs. E. Colman, Mr. G. Flaunty, Alan and Julie Seymour, Vanessa Mann (Jaywick Library), and Mr. Davies and Mr. Violin of Frobisher School. I am also grateful to staff at Colchester Record Office, Mrs. S. Reader (Clacton Library) members of the Clacton Historical Society, staff at the East Essex Gazette, Clacton Police publicity and personnel department, Glenda Selwood, Dave, Bob, Wyn, Ray and Brenda Oliver, E. Phillips, Mr. B. Matthews, Mr. N. Stedman, the Freeholders Association, Mrs. J. Fluin, Mrs. P. Wilding (New Tendring Clacton Council—Publicity Department), Mr. Roy Smith, Mr. and Mrs. Inch, Fran and Den, Sharon, Josie and Roy, Mr. Druce (The Ratepayers), Mr. D. Taylor, Kate and Ernie, Mr. K. Walker, Mr. N. Jacobs, Mr. David Shipman, and the residents of Jaywick. They spent time with me and loaned me photographs; without their help this book could not have been written.

Foreword

Just as everyone has his or her story, so too does every place. The story of Jaywick goes back to prehistory, but the story of Jaywick Sands is still within living memory of a small and fast declining number. Mrs. Lyons has undertaken the task, not a moment too soon, of recording that story.

There are council records and newspaper files to refer to, but she has been able to 'put flesh on the bones' of the written record by talking to some of the personalities that were involved, from the beginning, or very near it, in the trials and tragedies, successes and celebrations that have taken place in Jaywick over the last 75 years or more. This will not be possible for much longer.

As a grandson of F.C. (Foff) Stedman, Jaywick Sands has been part of my own life story from earliest childhood, and I am intrigued to discover parts of the story with which I was not familiar. I am sure that others will also, and I hope that some will be encouraged to add, in their own way, their recollections and contribute to the story of Jaywick Sands.

Neil C. Stedman
1996

Dedicated to the heroes of the 1953 flood disaster and my own hero Joe.

O GOD OUR HELP IN AGES PAST
OUR HOPE FOR YEARS TO COME
OUR SHELTER FROM THE STORMY BLAST
AND OUR ETERNAL HOME.

[Extract from hymn sung at first church service held in Jaywick, Sunday 31 July 1932]

Introduction

I fell in love with Jaywick Sands in the early 1960s after renting a timber-built holiday home there for £6 a week. Water was drawn from a standpipe on the side of a road, and the loo was an 'Elsan chemical' situated at the back.

Joe my husband howled 'It's Over' along with Roy Orbison as we motored from London in our three-wheeled white bubble car, called Caroline by our dear nephew Gary.

I wore mini-skirts and shiny knee-high boots. Joe wore leather, had long greasy hair and looked tough. Our evenings were spent in Brooklands Club or The Morrocco Café; our days were spent crabbing from a pillbox at Lion Point, lazing on the yellow soft sands, and racing in and out of the waves. Sadly, it's now all over for Roy Orbison, but not for Jaywick; it remains the same, only different. It is still a place in the sun where people enjoy life while the rest of the world goes by.

1 'Making waves' in 1935.

1

In the Beginning

Old Jaywick

Jaywick Sands Estate, a community of just over 4,000 residents, is a small modern bungalow seaside resort located two miles south west of Clacton-on-Sea on the Essex coastline. It appears on Chapman and André's Map of Essex in 1777 as Jewick. On recent maps it is still written as Jewick, but spellings differ.

The estate was founded in 1928, but the history of Jaywick goes back thousands of years. Once a fishing place for bishops and monks, and the haunt of bands of smugglers, it falls from West Road to rise again slightly near the sea wall. It has its highest point at the eastern end of Beach Road (renamed Broadway in 1953) and from the level of the ground dips towards Meadow Way, The

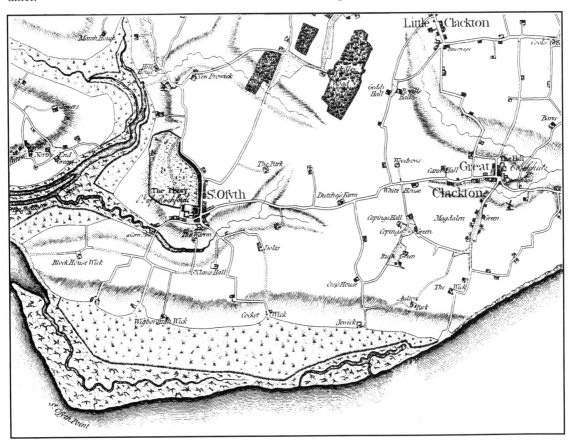

2 Chapman and André's map of 1777.

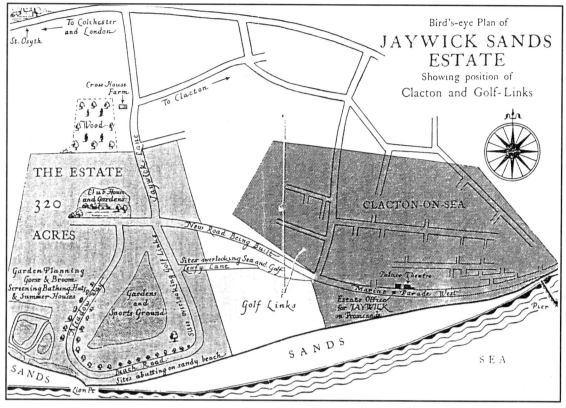

3   A plan of the estate in 1929.

Village, located between the Tudor Estate and the coast and Brooklands and Grasslands (New Town) which lies to the west of The Village.

The contours of the land were formed after the Ice Age over 30,000 years ago when melting ice left a pocket of water. When the North Sea was dry land Jaywick was no more than a watering-hole for prehistoric man. Once the largest in Great Clacton, the 320-acre farm was bordered on the west by a stream at Lion Point and Cockett Wick. Lion Point, 'Old Lion' (called 'the hump' locally), is the parish boundary between St Osyth and Great Clacton according to a memorandum of 1774.

On the east, the farm extended to East Wick, and was bounded to the north by small farms that replaced old woodlands. On the south it had a seaboard extending from Lion Point to Eastness, a distance of a mile. From the air, the outline of an old Roman villa can be observed to the left of West Road, near Jaywick Lane.

A mound found at Lion Point is thought to be an old salt workings. This, along with bones and relics unearthed in the area, supports the theory that there was a settlement of considerable size here long before the Romans came along. Several Celtic coins have been found in Jaywick, one by a local man working on the sea wall in 1973. This small gold coin, from the fifth or sixth century, was sold to Colchester Museum for £75. These coins can be viewed at Colchester and London museums.

Following the Roman evacuation a succession of invaders from the Continent settled in Britain. While Celts are believed to have established the community which became the village of Great Clacton, it is named after an early Saxon chieftain called Clacc. He settled there with his followers, and called the place Clackingawick, spelt Clakyngewyk in the earliest known record of 1438. Reduced to its component parts the name can be translated as 'dairy farm of the people of Clacc'. The spoken word has since softened it to Gewick and so to the present Jaywick.

St Osyth, originally called 'Chich', meaning creek, is a delightful village just three miles west of Jaywick. Here peacocks attract visitors as well as peahens amid the wide lawns of the elegant priory, one of the finest monastic buildings in the country. The ivy-clad building, home today to Mr. Somerset and Lady Juliet de Chair, was once used as an Essex learning and charity centre. It was founded by Richard de Belmeis, Bishop of London, in the 11th century.

Among its many attractions is one of the world's greatest masterpieces: a lifesize portrait of the stallion 'Whistlejacket', painted in 1762 by George Stubbs. There are also the 19th-century Rose and Water Gardens and a 13th-century chapel. In honour of one of the founders of Clacton Hospital, William H. Simpson, M.D., and his wife, the chapel has a beautiful stained glass window showing St Luke, the patron saint of physicians, holding a bunch of herbs.

In his very detailed book *The History of Clacton*, K. Walker records that prior to the Norman Conquest all of this part of Essex belonged to the Bishops of London. Being appendant to the manor of Great Clacton for many years, Jaywick was owned by successive Bishops of London until it was conveyed by Bishop Bonner to King Henry VIII in 1545 in exchange for other property. The king stripped it of its wealth and gave it to Cromwell. When this relationship turned sour and Cromwell went to the scaffold, the king installed Thomas Darcy in the priory. He was an ambitious cousin of Queen Jane Seymour and ten years later was created Baron Darcy. After the king died, the priory and local estates passed to his daughter Mary. By May 1553, Darcy had possession; it had been granted to him along with several other local properties. Although for a time it was thought to have been conveyed to a Henry Wyndham, it remained with the Darcy family for about three-hundred years. It eventually came to Elizabeth, Countess Rivers in her own right, the daughter of Thomas the 3rd Earl Darcy. During the Civil War this rich and powerful woman, because of her position and faith, was imprisoned for debts. Before her

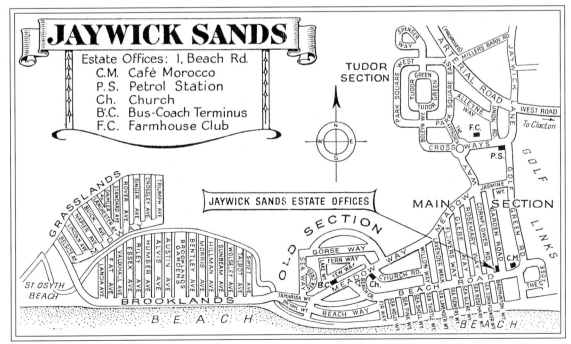

4   A map showing Jaywick Sands estate in the 1960s. On the left is Brooklands and in the centre is the beach hut section. In the right forefront is The Village.

capture she somehow managed to put her estates into trust. A number were sold in 1659 to Richard Scutt and William Watts, both of Westminster, to pay off debts—one was Jaywick.

The farm then came to a succession of landowners and tenant farmers: Mr. John Brown was the last of these. According to records in 1778 one tenant, James Maskall, became a landowner and farmer of great wealth and repute. He gave the land in the Old Road, Clacton, for two almshouses to be allocated for the aged poor of Clacton. Buried in St John's churchyard, Great Clacton, his tomb can still easily be identified.

In 1662 the old farm was sold for £2,300 by Watts, the trustees of Scutt, to Benjamin Rous, the occupier. It then passed to his son Robert who sold it in 1684 to the trustees of Bernard Whalley of the Middle Temple. He sold it in 1689 to Philip Gardiner, a citizen of London, and apothecary of Wapping who left it to his daughter Elizabeth who in turn left it to her mother, Frances, with the remainder to her sister and trustees. When the sister and

5 To the beach, and the Martello tower can just be seen in the background, 1933.

trustees died before Frances in 1721, Jaywick was seized by distant cousins, the Garbutts. But other cousins contested their action and the case went to the Chancery, where it was decreed that the farm should be sold to comply with Elizabeth's will. The Garbutts' appeal against the decision failed. In June 1732 a Colchester tailor and freeman of the town, whose family was thought to come from Norfolk, Mr. George Wegg (sometimes confused with the notorious smuggler Captain Wegg) bought the farm for £1,600.

In addition George bought Millars Barn, located near the junction of Jaywick Lane, an ancient roadway. He also bought Crossway House in the same area where Catherine, the wife of General Booth who founded the Salvation Army, died of cancer on 4 October 1890.

During the 18th century James Round married into the family which owned Jaywick. Soon he was acting as their agent. Charles Gray Round, his grandson, inherited the farm along with other properties including Colchester Castle. He owned nearly three miles of coastline and foreshore, and in 1851 purchased Wash Farm. Its land extended from Jaywick and continued in a string of narrow fields on the clifftop as far as what became Connaught Gardens. When Charles died in 1867, he left the estates in trust. It came to his nephew, James Round, the local Conservative M.P. from 1868 until 1906. James sold some of his land, but the Martello Tower, owned by the War Office, blocked his fields to the west. He made available an area for use as a recreation ground and gave part of the land for the building of St James' Church as well as the site for Clacton Hospital.

In 1895 he secured land in front of the Martello Tower to enable the Marine Parade to be extended. This area, Wash Lane, known as Round's estate, was sold by his trustees two years after he died in 1916. In 1920 the land was put up for sale for £8,500. When Mr. Frank Christopher Stedman, the founder of Jaywick Sands estate, came into the picture in 1928, a Mrs. Tweedi was in possession. Stedman paid £7,500 for the land.

2

The Jaywick Decision

Lord of the Manor

Stedman, a silver-haired flamboyant man with a great sense of humour, an eternal cockeyed optimist, was called 'Foff' or 'F.C.' by his friends. He had fierce blue eyes and a winning, persuasive personality. His many interests included painting, reading and local history. A devoted family man, he had six children and lived on Alleyn Road, West Dulwich, south-east London, with his dark-haired wife Elizabeth (Minnie to friends).

Madly in love, the young couple married without telling their families—only the bride's uncle was let in on the secret. He gave his niece away at St Mary's Church, Algate (now demolished), on 17 November 1894.

Throughout his life bad weather appeared to dog Stedman's footsteps, even on his wedding day. It was so cold that the Thames had frozen over, and the pair of lovebirds spent their wedding day huddled in Madame Tussaud's trying to keep warm.

By 1928, Stedman was working as a land agent and surveyor for a very large London concern; he had been just 12-years-old when he first got involved in this line of business. During the 1920s he developed 13 other estates involving 3,575 acres and 84 miles of roads. His purchase of Elmer on the south coast made him lord of the manor. After dividing each estate into building plots he sold them. Although he was never directly involved in building himself, he did impose restrictive covenants on all his estates as to the size of the plots and houses.

Frost had painted the trees silver on the cold January morning Stedman manoeuvred his

6 Frank Christoper Stedman, seen here in 1934, was the founder of the estate.

car through London to drive the 90-minute journey to view the farm. Soft whirling snow-flakes greeted his arrival.

Parking on Meadow Way, for centuries a simple cart track and the only road on the estate that led to Lion Point, he set off to view what was now mostly reclaimed marshland, dykes, and windswept sand dunes flanking the North Sea (once called the German Ocean). Across the saltings, near Lion Point, a stream flowed

7 Mrs. E. Stedman (sitting) in 1934, surrounded by her family.

8 The Stedmans and Lansburys at Foff's Corner.

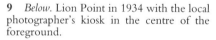

9 *Below.* Lion Point in 1934 with the local photographer's kiosk in the centre of the foreground.

seawards, dividing into two near the wall. The whole area was under the jurisdiction of Clacton Urban District Council. (I shall refer to the Clacton Urban District Council as the council throughout this book.)

A herd of prize friesian cows included in the sale grazed contentedly on the bleak marsh. By summer this landscape would be filled with wild flowers and birds feeding on berries.

Stedman, the man who would change Jaywick forever, watched gulls swooping low on the deserted beach used extensively during the 18th and 19th centuries by gangs of smugglers. Before then, in the Middle Ages, men had fished using wooden weirs built to catch the fish as the tide ebbed. This bounty earned money for the Bishops of London and the beach formed part of their stipend. It is still possible, at low tide, to see the relics of the old weirs, called 'keddalls', which during Elizabethan times were considered bad for shipping.

The January lead-grey sky was dreary and dull as the sea, but due to his background Stedman knew he had picked the ideal time to view. There was no bright golden sunshine or sweet-smelling blooms to enchant and fool him; he saw Jaywick at its worst, but could easily imagine it at its best.

An attractive 18th-century farmhouse situated to the rear of Crossways (near West Road) stood close to a farm-worker's cottage that was later turned into a popular café. Situated close by were a pair of cottages called 'Seaspray' and 'Sunnyside' belonging to Mrs. P. Farrant, a widow. Stedman later purchased these to make way for his development.

The oldest property in the area was a charming cottage called 'Seabright'. This had a thatched roof and was over three-hundred years old. When this cottage was demolished in the 1960s to make way for Jaywick Methodist Church, some Elizabethan wall paintings were exposed beneath the plaster. The rubble of the cottage was used in the foundations of the church.

There was also a small petrol station at Crossways, privately-owned and managed by the Harris family (today called Golf Green Garage). Three local shops, including Dot's

Tuck Shop, owned and managed by Mr. Frank Allum, an astute businessman, were located in the centre of The Village. This was the section of Jaywick which had already been laid out, and it served 100 or so residents living permanently in the area. Stedman made on that day what he called afterwards 'the Jaywick decision'. He purchased the farm and Jaywick Sands, his baby, had arrived.

Spade Work

With a head filled with schemes, Stedman set about realising a dream, handling his affairs in a firm but friendly fashion. He had the reputation of being a hard, sometimes crafty, businessman—it was said his left hand never knew what his right was doing.

We can supply all your Requirements.
Large and Complete Stocks.

High-Class Confectionery, Tobacco and Cigarettes, Stationery. Post Cards Novels, Etc.

"Dot's" Tuck Shops

Prop.: Frank O. Allum.

63, Beach Way and 8, Beach Road.

JAYWICK.   Telephone: CLACTON 798.

Daily and Weekly Newspapers. Toys, Fancy Goods, everything for the Beach and Holiday Time.

Films Supplied, Developed and Printed.
Expert and Rapid Service.

The Clacton Times

and East Essex Gazette

is

Jaywick's Weekly Paper

and is on Sale at Jaywick every Friday morning

Price 1d.

Printers and Publishers: A. QUICK AND CO., LTD.,
Times Buildings, Clacton-on-Sea

10   Advertisements from 1935.

11 *Above.* Cottages at Crossways in 1928.

12 *Left.* Jaywick's 18th-century farmhouse had its own tennis courts and tea rooms and was located to the rear of Crossways, on the edge of the estate. It was converted into a social club by Mr. Stedman, and after a merger with the Freeholders in 1934, it became their headquarters. It was demolished in 1984 and a block of flats has since been built on the site at Donna Drive.

13 *Below.* Golf Green Garage at Crossways in 1936. It has seen several owners over the years, but it was owned by the Harris family in 1928 when the estate was founded. It is still a thriving concern.

14 *Above.* The first houses to be built by Stedman on Golf Green Road, The Village, in 1929.

15 *Right.* Cyclists on Golf Green Road in 1933.

Stedman always involved and shared his luck, good or bad, with his family. Jack, his eldest, David, Reginald, Ivy, Olive and Ida all became involved in 'the Jaywick decision'. Reginald and David helped to control the estate after Jack was installed as resident estate manager in an office on the promenade at Clacton, while all local enquiries were dealt with at 'Dot's'.

The landscape changed overnight as bull-dozers, excavators and tractors replaced the old wooden farm machinery. The contractors, all local, got stuck in, such as Canlan & Sons Ltd., who tackled a new concrete road, a continuation of Marine Parade West. They laid some 3,000 feet of concrete in only seven weeks, well ahead of schedule. The road linked the estate with Clacton. Golf Green Road and Beach Road, the estate's main thoroughfare, followed.

At the same time an artificial lake was under construction at Lion Point, while behind the golf links, which together with an airstrip separated Jaywick from Clacton, six houses and a bungalow were being erected.

Meanwhile Stedman faced serious problems. Clacton councillors, although making him welcome, rejected his disposal works for main drainage because of the threat of flooding and the area's low-lying position. Stedman argued that because the land was 16 feet above low water mark, it must drain off again, and that even if there were floods, the drainage would be there forever. However, the council believed the land to be unsuitable for permanent houses, favouring the area now the Tudor Estate as more suited to that purpose.

Because during the earlier part of the 19th century there had been increasing concern throughout the country for the health and welfare of the people, citizens of large and small towns formed themselves into special commissions to deal with sanitation, paving and lighting. Following several Public Health Acts these functions were extended to rural areas.

When Great Clacton Urban Council and the Tendring Rural District Council were created—the prefix Great was soon dropped—there were 12 councillors and three wards. Today there are 60 councillors and 32 wards. From 1899 until 1949 the council provided electricity, water and gas. Among its most important duties as a Public Health Authority was the provision of sewers.

Promoting the Estate

Stedman kept his problems with the council under his hat, and on 18 May 1929 he published his intentions for the estate in a glowing front-page advertisement in the local newspaper:

Plots with an equal amount of land for a car or garden could be had for £25.00; better sites for £100 and £200. A house or chalet could be built for £395 to £850. West of Lion Point was thought suitable for bathing houses that could be built for £25.00 or hired. [This area subsequently became the Brooklands and Grasslands section (New Town).]

The estate would be built in two sections, one for beach huts the other for chalets and houses. Whenever possible local labour and business people would be employed. An artifical lake, one mile long and a half mile wide, was in the course of construction. It would provide motor boat racing and other attractions. Main drainage and good concrete roads would be provided by the Estate.

Jaywick Sands Estate

Price List *of Beach Chalets*

TYPE		
No. 1	£20	0
No. 2	£36	0
No. 3	£49	10
No. 5	£49	10
No. 6	£49	10
No. 7	£59	10
No. 8	£59	6
No. 9	£69	10
No. 10	£69	10
No. 11	£79	10
No. 12	£89	10
No. 15	£63	0
No. 16	£89	0
No. 17	£75	0
No. 18	£75	0
No. 19	£68	0
No. 20	£93	0
No. 21	£100	0

The Estate Builder will be pleased to quote prices for any modification on these designs or on any special plan a purchaser may prefer. Prices for extras such as leaded light windows, lining the huts with three-ply wood or insulating board, built-in furniture, bunks, cupboards, etc., can be had on application.

The Estate Architect will be pleased to prepare special plans to the requirements of purchasers.

JAYWICK SANDS ——ESTATE——

Adjoining Clacton-on-Sea Golf Links

FREEHOLD BEACH HUTS SITES

20 Feet Frontage, 50 Feet Deep

£30

All with Direct Access for Cars

∎

FINE CONCRETE ROADS

FACES FULL SOUTH

16 Advertisement for chalets and sites on the Jaywick Sands estate in the 1930s.

17 Exhibition stand at Gidea Park, Romford, in 1933.

18 Another shot of the exhibition stand at Gidea Park.

19 Model chalets at Olympia in 1936.

20 Exhibition stand at Olympia in the mid-1930s.

21 Advertisement for the flooding of the Lake in 1929.

Come to Jaywick

to see the

FLOODING of the GREAT LAKE

a

MILE LONG

By a huge pump, pumping 600,000 gallons per hour, now in progress.

Then have Tea at the

Jaywick Tea Rooms

DANCING from 4 p.m.

or

Spend the Afternoon on the finest stretch of
SANDY BEACH IN THE DISTRICT.

Take

Yellow (Enterprise) Bus from Town or Jetty

Which run EVERY HALF HOUR

Right to the

Jaywick Sands Estate

The estate was represented at the Model Houses Exhibition, Gidea Park, in 1933. Salmon & Son, a Clacton concern, designed the exhibition models. In 1935 14 were displayed constantly at the Ideal Homes Exhibition, Olympia, all fully furnished and displayed on a floodlit stand with a background painted to depict the golden sand at Jaywick. The attractive stand was designed by Mr. Johnson, Stedman's sales manager.

Adverts frequently appeared in daily and weekly London newspapers, including *The Daltons Weekly*.

The Clacton Sporting Lake Company

Clacton-on-Sea, population 50,000, is a popular seaside resort founded by Mr. Peter Schuyler Bruff, a professional engineer. At its peak, over 6,000 holiday-makers arrived each week to enjoy its amenities which included the West Cliff Theatre. It was packed that June of 1929 when Stedman teamed up with Mr. J.V. Bond, the owner of Cockett Wick Farm to the rear of Jaywick, to form the Clacton Sporting Lake Company Limited.

Butterflies and birds gently fluttered about masses of red and purple poppies covering the marsh when in July Stedman invited people, again via the local paper, to come to see the flooding of the lake. Afterwards tea was served at the old farmhouse, refurbished and opened for the first time that Whitsun weekend. Here they could, if they wished, dance from 4 p.m. onwards.

Jaywick, like Clacton, occupies a south-facing position and frequently enjoys up to 1,600 hours of annual sunshine. During that particular weekend temperatures soared into the nineties and this, together with the advert, lured visitors to the area. Wearing beach clothes and sun-shades, they came along to watch a 22-inch petrol-driven pump lift water over the sea wall into the lake at a rate of 600,000 gallons per hour. Hundreds of boats registered with the Clacton Outboard Racing Club; Stedman had good reason to believe the lake would be a success. Alas, there would be no future Torvill and Deans skating to the haunting beauty of Ravel's *Bolero* on this lake: as fast as the water went in, it drained away.

After this failure the company was sold to Stedman, through his daughter Mrs. Suffling as nominee. Four years later, on 20 July 1933 Stedman conveyed the sea wall and dykes to Mrs. Robinson, another daughter. Together Grasslands and Brooklands form New Town. This area was part of the then Tendring Rural District Council which agreed to the development of some 800 plots there. (The Tendring Rural District Council is referred to as Tendring Rural throughout this book.)

Here stood a Martello Tower, one of 10 on the coastline between St Osyth and Walton. Squat and round, these buildings were part of the seaside outlook for years and stretched from near Clacton at the mouth of the Thames estuary to Aldeburgh in Suffolk. They guarded some of the most isolated river mouths and marshes in the country. All east coast towers, built when invasion by the French was imminent, were recognised by the letters of the alphabet.

Jaywick's Martello Tower stood near an ancient sluice that allowed the marshlands and dykes to discharge at low tide. This and a wall that stretched round to St Osyth beach were once maintained by landowners, but were usually badly neglected. They were for a time improved and maintained by the Level Commissions, although eventually this responsibility passed to the former Maldon, Wivenhoe and Clacton Drainage board whose functions were in turn taken over by the Essex River Authority, along with the levying of the necessary rates.

22 Flooding the Great Lake. Stedman wrote on the postcard, 'The "Great Lake" at Jaywick another blighted hope—such is life'.

23 Gang working at the lake site, 1929.

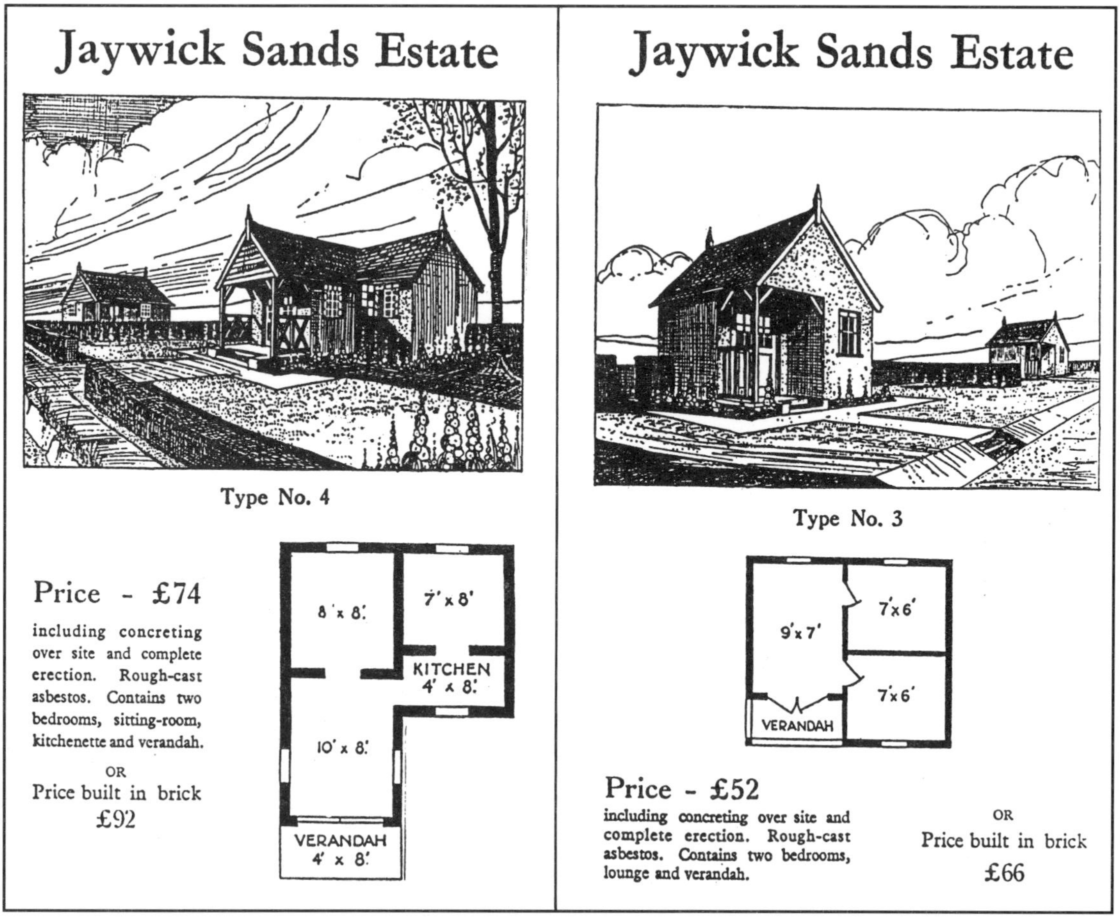

Jaywick Sands Estate

Type No. 4

Price - £74

including concreting over site and complete erection. Rough-cast asbestos. Contains two bedrooms, sitting-room, kitchenette and verandah.

OR
Price built in brick
£92

8' x 8'.　　7' x 8'.

KITCHEN
4' x 8'.

10' x 8'.

VERANDAH
4' x 8'.

Jaywick Sands Estate

Type No. 3

9' x 7'　　7' x 6'

7' x 6'

VERANDAH

Price - £52

including concreting over site and complete erection. Rough-cast asbestos. Contains two bedrooms, lounge and verandah.

OR
Price built in brick
£66

24　Property specifications in 1935.

Blazing autumn leaves of brown russet, scarlet and gold blasted along the leafy lanes when Stedman again approached the council. He was armed with alternative plans for drainage but to his disappointment these too were rejected.

Cutting his losses, Stedman abandoned altogether the idea at this stage. He put cesspools into those houses already built, and sold four of them at a loss. He allowed his son Reginald to live in the bungalow, and Mr. Webb, his foreman, to live in the remaining house. Plans were then submitted to the council for what were described as beach huts. Stedman thought they would be sanctioned under the by-laws concerning tents, caravans and huts. The plans were passed.

The Estate

The farm was developed in four sections. The first was Brooklands, to the west of Lion Point, and this was followed by Grasslands, to the rear of the estate where a dirt road runs along the back of the sea wall. This is called Snakes Lane locally because common grass snakes nest in the rushes. A notice warning people of their existence has gone. These harmless adders, unlike the poisonous ones that are easily distinguished by the chain of dark spots running along their spine, often slip over to Brooklands for a drink in the dykes during hot summers. Together these sections became New Town or the Tendring Section.

Brooklands was named by Stedman, for undisclosed personal reasons, but it is generally believed that all the avenues were named after famous motor-car manufacturers—Morris Avenue, Austin Avenue, Triumph Avenue etc.—because the motor-car had played such a large part in the success of the estate.

'The Beach Hut' section, the third section, is known locally as The Village and is located at the lower end of Meadow Way. This leads to a beach where at the beginning of the century a rifle range was located. This fell into disuse after the First World War.

Here small chalets were built behind others in a 'tandem' arrangement. They were mostly brick built, and the first beach hut ever built on the estate was on Meadow Way. Sites measuring 20ft. x 26ft., with a 40ft. frontage sold for £48

while bungalows on stilts, on a freehold site measuring 20ft. x 50ft. cost in total £52. Those huts which were built on single plots contained two rooms measuring 9ft. x 7ft. and 7ft. x 6ft., together with a deep verandah.

The walls were covered with tongued and grooved weather boarding, and roofs with rock-faced Anderson's Rok-Flextile in two colours. They were finished externally in two colours of Solignum. Temporary building permits were obtained to build them.

The roads are named after flowers and shrubs found in a cottage garden: Jasmine Way, Cornflower Way, Gorse Way, and Rosemary Way, for example. (For convenience I shall refer to this section as The Village throughout this book.)

25 Morris Avenue, Brooklands, in 1935.

26 The dyke dividing Grasslands and Brooklands, 1935.

27   The stocks and wishing well on the Tudor Estate, 1936.

The Tudor Estate, the fourth and last section, is located to the north of Jaywick, facing West Road. It is the first section seen on arrival, and was Stedman's pride and joy.

Purpose-built, it was the only area built for all-year-round occupation along the lines of conventional town planning. Here two-bedroomed houses cost £323 and plots measuring 30ft. x 145ft. cost from £130 to £170.

It had a central green of six acres. This open space contained a stock, a pillory and a wishing well. Elizabethan links with Jaywick were reflected in the road names: Spencer Way, Frobisher Drive, Aragon Close and so on.

Because in the early days some bank managers or building societies believed all property in Jaywick was beach huts, customers often had trouble getting a mortgage. To overcome the problem and so speed up sales local builders such as Wiggins Ltd. would speak of West Clacton, as opposed to Jaywick, in their sales literature. Many residents living in the section still believe this is not Jaywick and refer to living in West Clacton.

Water was supplied through meters, and was collected in pails from standpipes on the side of the road. Because there was no piped water or main drainage on the rest of the estate,

at the back of the avenues rows of little out-houses were built to accommodate Elsan toilets. These were pails placed inside wooden seat frames which had to be emptied manually.

Stedman employed various sanitary companies for this task whose employees were nicknamed 'The Bisto Kids'. A tank on wheels called the 'Honey Cart' was pulled by two horses called, would you believe, Bugger and Sod!

Converted Lancaster Bomber petrol carriers called 'The Bowsers' replaced the 'Honey Carts' after the war, and employees worked 12-hour a day shifts starting at around 4 a.m. A metal disc displayed outside each hut carrying the letter 'J' indicated when 'The Sentry Box', as they were referred to, was occupied.

Strips of fly paper were hung inside to ward off the assortment of insects these toilets always attracted. Hair wound round curlers, flanked by a row of crocodile clips was also used. One old-timer cried with laughter remembering bluebottles buzzing about: 'they were as big as swallows', she insisted.

Honeysuckle, blackberrry blossom, tall purple foxgloves, sweet pea and winter jasmin roamed at will, even covering the building which housed the equipment and horses used by the sanitary collectors.

3

The Children of Jaywick

The Freeholders

Thousands of people from all over the country purchased holiday homes on the estate, but it was the East Enders—called the 'Children of Jaywick' by Stedman—who carried the torch. Famous all over the world for their ways and sayings, these people came from the docking sections of Stepney, Poplar, East and West Ham. These were areas which attracted thousands of foreign sailors and people of different nationalities.

Among them were Polish Jews who had come to England to escape religious persecution. Thousands hailed from the land of leprechauns and begorras, Ireland, leaving behind them the distress of the potato famine. 'Walking back to Happiness' singer, Helen Shapiro, was born in Bethnal Green, the heart of cockney London. The Rt. Hon. George Lansbury, who came from Poplar, was once leader of the Labour Party, and became a personal friend of Stedman. Fred Pontin, who turned a £23,000 investment in a derelict training camp into a £55 million international leisure industry, came from Shoreditch and Dame Vera Lynn, 'The Force's Sweetheart', was born in East Ham.

Jaywick, with its yellow sand, dancing blue sea and healthy air, was a far cry from the grime of city life. It represented freedom to a generation coping with the pain of the Great War. Grabbing Stedman's offer with both hands these small freeholders, mostly neighbours and friends, arrived in dribs and drabs at the estate.

28 Mr. G. Lansbury M.P. at Foff's Corner in 1934.

A breed apart, boredom was never part of their world. They built their own little homes with their own money, without the benefit of planners or building societies even though local builders offered to do so within a week for £20.

Owning their own place in the sun was their own 'Golden Apple'. People brought building materials on cars, vans and even bicycles. By 1931 about two-hundred little huts and chalets dotted the coastline in a higgledy-piggledy fashion.

With the growing estate lacking any official road numbering system, plot-owners devised their own house names such as 'Lazy Days', 'Windy Way', 'Whoopee' and 'Finnigan's Rainbow'. These were hung or nailed with pride on and over the doors. Looking neat and pretty as doll's houses, the homes were painted the colours of the rainbow. Beach pyjamas were worn to match the colour of the property as well as the estate's car badge colours of blue and yellow.

Everything was new, young, and exciting. Youngsters loved to fetch pails of water from the dripping standpipes on the side of the avenues. Day-trippers carrying balls, rubber rings and fishing nets spent hours on the sun-drenched beach indulging sun-starved bodies, but the busy plot-owners stopped only to wave a warm hello. However, before a boil-red sun slipped into the sea, they usually found time to sit indoors or out on their verandahs, having a gossip or a sing-song.

Somebody was sure to whip out an accordion, banjo or mouth organ. Camp-fire songs and old favourites included 'My fiddle my sweetheart', 'I'm only a rough old diamond' and 'My old Mother In Law'. The latter was sung with gusto.

This was a world they loved; there was so much to do and see. Walks to Clacton along the sea-front led past the manicured lawns of the golf links, laid out in 1896 on 50 acres and bought by the council in 1951. During 1890 this area was considered by developers for a vast sports arena to include a golf course, and a race track, similar to the Brooklands of 1906.

Some £180,000 was required to implement the scheme, which relied heavily on road and rail transport links. It would have provided work for about 600 men but what materialised was the golf course and a yacht pond. A syndicate bought the bowls green site for Butlin's in 1922.

A Martello Tower was rented out for £45 per annum to a Mr. and Mrs. Maskell, who turned the accommodation—two sitting rooms, two bedrooms and a kitchen—into a cosy home for about 19 years. The nearby Tower Café sold tea, minerals and cakes on the road to Clacton. Here one could visit the attractive shops and the pier, watch paddle steamers trail along the coast on their way to London, or visit the 270-ft. long jetty. Built mainly for barges unloading building materials, after this structure was hit by a floating mine during the Second World War, it was blown up to prevent its use in any invasion of England.

A limited range of convenience stores opened up to sell food, whilst others rented out prams and cots. Most of the names involved have long since disappeared from the scene but 'Dot's' has survived.

Mr. Allum, Jaywick's coastguard for a time, expanded and opened several businesses in the area. These included a sub-post office and a chemist run by his brother Dennis, a local councillor in time. He at one stage ran a driving school from Beach Road.

Frank Allum's daughter Pam, along with her husband William, owns and manages the concern today. Brooklands Gardens became Brooklands main shopping thoroughfare and Beach Road (renamed Broadway in September, 1953) is the main street in The Village.

The first shop built on the estate was Grants, a general store. Mr. L. Doe, manager at a Clacton dairy, who kept a couple of horses on a field at Millars Barn, opened the Model Dairy Farm at Brooklands Gardens before moving on to Beach Road. This concern survived well into the 1990s until it was put up for sale by trustees. There was a butcher, Lloyd Johnson, and a grocer, F. Hale, on Beach Road.

No English holiday resort is complete without a fish and chip shop: Jaywick has several. Jaywick Fisheries opened in Brooklands Gardens but by 1934 had moved on to Beach Road in The Village. There the owner

29 Holiday-makers cavorting on the beach in 1933.

30 Two young holiday-makers in the early 1930s.

31 Holiday-makers posing for a photograph in 1935.

Mrs. Smith trained her pet monkey to sell tickets for fund-raising events outside. This bundle of fun had brains to burn, residents joked. It was a big attraction to youngsters who fussed over it and demanded—and usually got—fish and chips 'only from the shop where the greatest monkey in Jaywick lived'. (More like crafty monkey, rivals muttered, eyeballing clever Mrs. Smith.)

Messrs. W.E. Dennis and Sons opened an off-licence at Sea Glebe Way in 1935, only yards from the front, and despite initial objections it was a success.

A neat row of shops opened on the Tudor Parade during the 1960s. Over the years it has had a wool shop, a tobacconist, a café-cum-hairdresser's (once a fish and chip shop owned by Doll and Ernie Perry) and a sub-post office, today run by Mr. Patel. A butcher's is owned today by the ever-cheerful Terry.

In 1934 the Jaywick Traders Association was formed by shopkeepers Frank Allum, G. Flaunty, and Dennis & Sons to ensure fair and safe trading in the area.

To cope with the holiday-makers, by 1934 Sutton's Crossley and Eastern National ran a direct service from Victoria or Kings Cross to the coach station at Tamarisk Way, situated in the centre of the estate. By road, rail and sea the estate was readily accessible, especially from London. The Colchester by-pass, which opened in 1933, was a great boost for the many families in the area who for the first time now owned their own motor-car. Austin Sevens and Morris Minors cost just over £100, and there were ten times as many bicycles.

The *Crested Eagle* and *Laguna Belle*, paddle steamers, sailed daily between Tower Bridge and Clacton. Hillman's Airways had a service connecting with Hillman's coaches from all parts of London to Romford. From 1958 pleasure flights could be booked from a field on West Road.

This airstrip was used by flying ace Sir Alan Cobham to give many air displays in the 1930s, and more recently it has come in handy for the popular car boot sales and various fund-raising

32   Jaywick's first off-licence was built in 1935. Today it is called the *Never Say Die*.

33 *Above*. Beach Road in the summer of 1935, with Jaywick Fisheries on the right.

34 *Right*. Beach Road corner, The Village, in the 1930s.

35 *Right*. Beach Way, The Village, in the 1960s. The 'Model Dairy Farm' foremost on the right of the picture was a popular dairy that survived well into the 1990s until it was sold by the trustees of Mr. Doe, the original owner of Clacton Dairy.

SUTTON'S CROSSLEY COACHES

Telephone 173   54 PIER AVENUE, CLACTON-ON-SEA   Telephone 173

PERIOD
RETURN
FARE:

9/6

To approx.
Whitsun.

Slight increase
in fare during
Summer period.

Please write
for
Handbills.

Seats can
be booked
at any Coach
Booking
Office
in London.

Children
half fare.

Suttons

THROUGH SERVICES DAILY between
LONDON and JAYWICK SANDS

Depart KINGS CROSS Coach Station 9.0 a.m.   2.0 p.m.   6.30 p.m. | Depart ILFORD   9.47 a.m.   2.47 p.m.   7.17 p.m.
    „   STRATFORD -   -   -   9.35 a.m.   2.35 p.m.   7.5 p.m. | Depart ROMFORD 10.1 a.m.   3.1 p.m.   7.31 p.m.
                    Depart JAYWICK 8.30 a.m., 2.0 p.m. and 6.30 p.m.

36 Advertisement for Sutton's Crossley Coaches, 1931.

37 A 1930s view of the golf links, adjoining the estate. It was laid out in 1896 and purchased by the local council in 1951. During 1890, the area was considered by developers for a vast sports arena to include a golf course and a race track similar to Brooklands. Finance became a problem and only the links and a yachting pond materialised. A syndicate bought the bowls green site for Butlin's in 1922.

charities. On Bonfire Night hundreds of rockets and squibs head towards the sky in a blare of noise.

At peak holiday times youngsters, usually as brown as berries and wearing swimsuits, hung about with wooden home-made wheel-barrows at the coach station offering to carry holiday-makers' luggage for a small tip. These barrows, made from used sugar boxes, were pushed over the 'hump'—a slope that separates New Town from the rest of the estate. They had big wheels rescued from old Victorian prams that creaked and threatened to buckle all the way; many collapsed in an untidy heap. But for those that made it there was a generous tip to spend in

the amusement arcades filled with games and rides. Other favourite pastimes included crabbing from Lion Point, sailing on *Beryl* a pleasure boat, or playing rounders on the beach.

Yellow 'top deck' coaches of the Enterprise Company, later absorbed into the present Eastern National, ran excursions from Jaywick to places of interest about the estate: Frinton-on-Sea, a pretty resort with a glorious greensward; Brightlingsea, a celebrated yachting and fishing centre; Colchester, famous for oysters, roses and Roman remains; Flatford Mill, Dedham, the scene of many of John Constable's paintings; and of course St Osyth, the 'Old World' village, with its priory and tales of witch trials during 1582.

4

A Circle of Happiness

Seaside resorts have always attracted people wanting to set up hotels and guest-houses, and in Clacton they were the most influential lobby. They hated the Jaywick estate growing up about them, seeing it as a threat to their livelihood.

Stedman carried on regardless and had more plans for beach huts passed in 1930 on the assurance that they were 'not to be used for sleeping in'. His attention was drawn to rumours that people were in fact sleeping in the huts by the Town Clerk who said he might have to take action as a result of pressure from the town. The council sent a medical officer down to the estate who saw several huts and said: 'I see these are being used for sleeping in! If they are used for that, ventilation must be put in and other things done.' These recommendations were carried out.

The plot-owners continued to maintain and paint their homes each year; the sea air just ripped the paint off. During the days leading up to Easter the little estate buzzed with activity.

Entertainment was usually self-made. Children played with bicycle wheels with or without spokes and hubs. Adults formed what they called 'A Circle of Happiness'. This cost 6d. to join and a new circle was started every 100 members. The money collected was used to provide entertainment for the children.

Organised outdoor games and debates were held on the Café Green which was located outside the Beach Café—a converted army hut used in the First World War. This was one of a pair which Stedman had bought from the council and in turn sold to the Freeholders Association. They were used as the Town Hall for eight years before the new Town Hall was designed by Sir Arthur Brumwell Thomas, also the designer of Belfast City Hall.

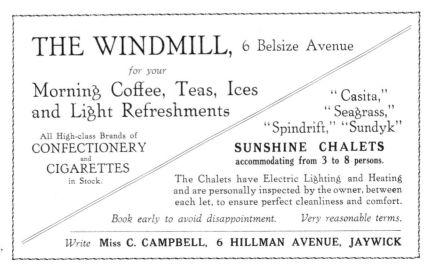

THE WINDMILL, 6 Belsize Avenue

for your

Morning Coffee, Teas, Ices and Light Refreshments

All High-class Brands of
CONFECTIONERY
and
CIGARETTES
in Stock.

" Casita,"
" Seagrass,"
" Spindrift," "Sundyk"

SUNSHINE CHALETS
accommodating from 3 to 8 persons.

The Chalets have Electric Lighting and Heating and are personally inspected by the owner, between each let, to ensure perfect cleanliness and comfort.

Book early to avoid disappointment.   *Very reasonable terms.*

Write **Miss C. CAMPBELL, 6 HILLMAN AVENUE, JAYWICK**

38 Jaywick advertisement, 1935.

23

39 Mr. P. Marsh, also known as 'Uncle Peter', seen on the right with his back to the camera, organised beach games in Brooklands during 1935.

40 'Uncle Peter' holds physical training classes, Café Green, in 1935.

41   G. Lansbury M.P., with members of the 'Circle of Happiness'.

While children screamed at Mr. Punch as he waved his stick and threw yet another 'wobbly', at the Punch and Judy show on the beach, Mum and Dad would take part in the outdoor debates organised on the Café Green. 'How to be happy even though you are married' was a subject sure to 'wind them up' as they sat on the grass, or on very hot days, in the sea. Meanwhile some played cards on tables set up in the sea, tucking into ice-cream and fizzy drinks, while others stayed on the beach and enjoyed sausage and mash, fish and chips, or saveloys and pease-pudding on sale at the Beach Café.

Stedman soon got caught up in the happy carefree atmosphere these people created. He provided evening entertainment in a marquee he erected on the green and hired a local trio called 'The Jolly Three Jays' to play at weekends. The entrance fee was 10d. and 6d. and he and his family watched and admired Jaywick's 'bright young things' dancing quicksteps and foxtrots.

The trio, dressed in their best, were very popular with the crowd. After tooting, whistling and cracking jokes, with a one, two, three they were off and the dancing began.

Bonnie baby competitions were held regularly so the parents could show off their little darlings. 'Come as you please Concerts', aimed at local talent and judged by the holiday-makers, were organised. Everybody was welcome except those daft enough to render their version of 'The Sailor on the Burning Deck', who suffered the taunts of 'let 'm burn!' from a thoroughly fed-up audience who dreaded poems of any sort. 'The Green Eye of The Little Yellow God' fared much better with the audience who felt sorry for 'Mad Carew' and the 'Colonel's daughter'.

Rotten weather became an excuse for organised singing in the marquee. Thunder and lightning rolled across the heavens but stood no chance against rousing sing-songs or 'My Old Mother in Law'!

42-44 Jaywick Beach Café, one of a pair of converted army huts was used as Jaywick's town hall for eight years and was the venue for the Freeholders' meeting in 1931. The Brooklands Club was built at the back.

The Freeholders Association

By now the ambitious plot-owners wanted better conditions on the estate. However, getting no response to their requests from the council, they decided to form their own association which became in every way a properly constituted council, bar official recognition. The first chairman was Mr. J. Coghill. Membership began at 2s. 6d. per annum. By the late 1930s it had risen to 10s. and today it costs £15. I shall refer to the Freeholders Association as the Freeholders throughout this book.

The association was formed primarily to provide a service for the owners of the few bungalows built in New Town. Established by 1931, it had a sports committee which organised dances and whist drives. It created several companies and sub-committees to handle the various needs of the estate. Jaywick Properties Company Limited, indirectly owned by the Freeholders, replaced the old association. A second company was created for the purpose of conducting the business enterprises of the association.

They purchased the Beach Café for £1,000 and the Café Green for £1,500 from Stedman, who included in the price the club premises and all the land from the tennis courts to Brooklands in 1934.

A council of management hired out the green and café, and the old farmhouse became the association's headquarters. The association took full responsibility for sanitary facilities, water supply, and maintenance on the estate. It held seasonal parties and annual London reunions which were usually packed. At its first annual meeting in the Beach Café in 1931 over 200 people attended. Among several issues raised at this meeting was the question of post—at this stage it was still left at the estate office for collection even though all the homes had numbers and the roads were named. Members now wanted a normal postal service, a public telephone, gas, water, and electricity.

45   Holiday-makers at Brooklands beach in August 1935.

Jaywick Sands Freeholders Association Ltd.

Registered Office:
BROOKLAND GARDENS, JAYWICK

The Association was formed to promote and protect the social interests of all Freeholders. It has taken a large part in the development of Jaywick, and it invites all freeholders to take the opportunity of protecting their interests

THE ANNUAL SUBSCRIPTION is 5/-, which includes membership, and all the amenities of a fine Social Club.

Secretary:
Mr. E. J. LANSBURY.

Chairman:
Mr. H. T. HOBBS.

46 An advertisement for the Freeholders Association in the 1930s.

BROOKLANDS GARDENS, JAYWICK SANDS.

JULY 30th and AUGUST 1st
At 6.30 p.m.

PROGRAMME
OF
CONCERTS

Arranged by the Jaywick Sands Freeholder's Association
(Parks and Sports Committee)
Under the Direction of NIG NEWEY.

ADMISSION FREE

A Collection will be made in aid of the Jaywick Sands Freeholder's Association Improvement Fund.

PROGRAMME - - PRICE 2d.

47 A programme from the Freeholders' first concert in 1932.

48 A reunion dinner and dance was held on 25 February 1936. It was presided over by Miss Bowman, councillor for Finsbury. On the back row, third from the left, is Mr. H.T. Hobbs.

Plots, Plans and Promises

By the end of 1931 the Freeholders had obtained gas, water, a normal postal service, and a public telephone was being erected. Stedman, keen to see the estate get on, gave them £300 which formed half the £600 needed to lay the 2,500ft. mains for the bulk water supply. All was well until along with some plot-owners Stedman applied to the council for connection to its electricity supply. He offered £250 per annum as security and donated the poles and land for the kiosks, while the plot-owners also offered a small sum.

Council engineers estimated the work involved would cost £2,900 and prepared a scheme involving the installation of 1,050 yards of overhead cable and two transformers. Several councillors thought it a good business proposition and because they had already given the estate water and gas felt they could hardly refuse to supply electricity, especially as they were busy touting for such business at this time. However, Councillor Fenton-Jones moved an amendment

that the matter be referred back because the area was below high water level with no protection apart from existing sea defences, nor proper land drainage.

In the event not only did the council refuse to supply electricity but it also instructed its Public Health Committee to take certain action that could result in the huts having to come down. By January 1932 the council had approached the Freeholders in order to issue temporary licences to existing hut owners for a three-year period, which were to be renewable only if certain works were carried out.

The council revealed that all the huts were built contrary to its by-laws. It claimed that Stedman's plans had not made reference to the use of the huts for sleeping. Instead they had been described as comprising ladies' and gentlemen's dressing rooms, together with lounge or reading room; 128 out of 180 were passed by the council on this representation. It claimed that they were not used as beach huts but as domestic dwellings and the dispute continued for two years. Throughout this period Stedman continued to sell plots and to allow building on them.

This controversy angered the plot-owners and they insisted that in the future everything was to be put in writing. They argued that by implication, and in some cases writing, they had been given to understand that sleeping was permissible. They had been told plans were deposited with the council, but in fact this was only true in 50 per cent of cases.

At the following Easter meeting, held in a marquee situated near Yew Way, there was uproar. The plot-owners attacked Stedman, blaming him for putting them in this position. Stedman and the council, they knew, did not see eye to eye, but it was they who were suffering. The council, represented at these meetings, was roasted for accepting rates based on yearly residence. The committee, which believed that council's requirements were reasonable, had considered it their duty to accept them. However, ordinary members of the association insisted that the committee did not have the authority to speak on their behalf.

The sub-committee threatened to resign when a resolution to reject the licences on the grounds they were 'unfair and inequitable' was passed, but were persuaded to carry on. When the council said it had only heard of the Freeholders during December 1931, a member reminded them that there had been an article in the local paper during August about the association.

'You knew, you were asleep with your eyes wide open! Why say this now? Why didn't you say something before we went to the expense of building our huts?' Members wanted answers to these questions.

Meetings were seldom dull or boring. That this Easter meeting did not develop into a 'free-for-all' was due in no small measure to the skill of the chairman. In putting the case for the council Councillor A. Green was quick to remind everybody that the council had been invited to this meeting, and that its representatives 'understood the position, and only wanted to assist, but we need to be met half way'. 'Glad to see you' came a sing-song reply.

An amendment was finally moved, and seconded by Mr. A.A. Wolfe—who was to make his mark and become one of the association's best remembered members—that the council be asked to agree to delete the last part of the licence form: in effect this would ensure that the plot-owners did not have to pull their huts down. Chairman Hobbs, a large jolly-faced man with jet-black hair, maintained that by paying tax and rates they had acknowledged the council and its by-laws.

By that summer the council, believing the plot-owners to have been misled about the building regulations, was reluctant to exercise its powers. Thus the existing buildings were allowed to remain, provided certain conditions were followed in future. Stedman continued to deny misrepresentation, and wrote an open letter dated 31 March 1932 to the editor of the local paper in which he quoted extracts from his correspondence with the council:

> Council knew very well the huts were slept in. Letters were passed to this office from buyers interested in buying property on the estate, health officials had been sent down who asked for ventilation to be put in if they were being slept in, who made recommendations that were carried out. Council had invited him to send particulars of accommodation for four people to interested parties.

Then cunning as a fox, Stedman watched and waited.

When the council, towards the end of the year, in its efforts to cope with high unemployment in the area, sought assistance from local business people by asking if they would offer employment, Stedman pounced. On 19 November 1932 he placed a full-page advertisement addressed to the unemployed of Clacton in the local paper:

> The Jaywick Estate offered to employ 100 men on Sewer work all winter and 25 extra, 50 next Spring and consequent on the development there would be 900 bungalows erected employing 500 men for two whole years. But your 'wise' councillors rejected the plan, and you must remain on the objectionable dole; advise your 'wise' councillors to think again!

He had spent £8,000 on the development so far, and estimated that £135,000 alone was spent in Clacton by Jaywick people in 1932 plus rates.

When a complete drainage scheme estimated to cost £16,000 was considered for the estate, trouble again raised its ugly head. Promised £2,472, the Freeholders hoped to raise another £7,000 by charging £12 10s. per hut. Stedman believed that for everyone's sake the estate needed main drainage, so he offered £3,000 towards the cost. Moreover, he intended putting into the estate a swimming pool, a dance hall and tennis courts, with or without the support of the Freeholders.

There was always a certain reluctance on the part of the members when considering expensive improvements to the estate such as main drainage or better roads: in view of recent events they were concerned that the council might again intervene.

Meanwhile all types of vehicles drove on the estate at whatever speed and caused damage. The Freeholders, with no authority whatsoever, were powerless to prevent this and wanted to take over the control of the roads. Stedman agreed to do various works on the roads, but would not relinquish control to the Freeholders as he wanted to be in a position to negotiate with the authorities as one individual instead of having to represent a multitude of people.

He had contractors stand by to work on the roads when improvements, costing 1s. 6d. each hut, were agreed fair but then sent them home after members didn't even bother to reply to the correspondence on the matter. The Freeholders, who believed that their members would have paid after completion, could do nothing. The council meanwhile laid a six-inch main in Jaywick Lane and planned to lay further mains down Meadow Way.

Miss Jaywick, 1932

During 1931 a local councillor complained that: 'the pyjama in the streets is not a credit to Clacton, they are disgusting and vulgar, the police should be called in'. His comment was sparked off by two girls wearing men's trousers and was ignored by most people. But when a visitor had the gall to write to a national newspaper complaining that: 'all Essex girls are plain Janes!' the 'Essex Boys' rushed to their girls'

49   The first Miss Jaywick, Miss W. Shipfield, seen here in 1932.

defence and the first Miss Clacton Beauty Contest, to include Clacton and surrounding districts, was the outcome. Organised by the Clacton Press Ball, a sub-branch of the Union of Journalists, the winner would be crowned at the Clacton Carnival, a popular event that has taken place annually since 1922. Miss Winfred Shipfield of Austin Avenue was voted the first Miss Jaywick.

Jaywick's Lifeboats

A fantastic seasonal attraction such as the Clacton Carnival drew visitors year in year out, as did the golden sands at Jaywick, but there were accidents.

In July 1932 Stedman's sales manager, Mr. C. Johnson (who people said could sell snow to an Eskimo), saved a boy from drowning, and the boy's grateful father decided to donate his own boat—a converted speed-boat—as a lifeboat. He also made a gift of his well-equipped boathouse, which became a lookout tower, with changing rooms above.

50   The Freeholders' lifeboat, *Beryl*, alongside Brett's timber-built jetty in 1935.

This boat, left on the beach during the day, was manned at all times by at least one voluntary crew member of the Freeholders. It was called out when a small 14ft. sailing boat carrying three men and a woman capsized. Another lifeboat, Clacton's *Edward Z Dresden* which had been launched in 1929, was also summoned.

'Don't mind me, leave me alone ... save the men first', the woman involved insisted. Happily everybody was rescued, and afterwards the Jaywick boat gained recognition from the Lifeboat Institute.

Soon afterwards the Freeholders bought another boat for emergencies and erected a boathouse for it. This contained a luggage room for overnight parcels, a committee room, and a sales office for Mr. Johnson. They also bought the first boat for £450 when Mr. Cooper, its owner, died early in 1936. A flag day at Whitsun raised the cash.

That same year during August there was further drama when the marquee caught fire. People turned out of bed to help when orange and yellow flames, many leaping as high as 20ft. in the air, lit up the whole area. Hot embers showered down, stifling smoke blinded everybody and the red-eyed distraught trio lost all their clothes and equipment bar the piano. This was dragged out and left in the centre of the green. The fire brigade could do nothing, and the marquee burnt to the ground.

People stood about in groups, trying to comfort the trio. Suddenly out of the semi-darkness a man appeared dressed in bright yellow striped pyjamas and matching bedroom slippers. To their astonishment, he plonked his round body down at the piano, rolled up his sleeves and in a high squeaky voice warbled his version of 'Let's put out the lights and go to sleep'. Alas, the 'Jolly Three Jays', already miserable, failed to appreciate 'the yellow canary'—as the man was dubbed later—and neither did anyone else. He took flight, and was chased by holiday-makers.

Sightseers came along to view the after-math of the fire the following day but there was nothing to see. Plot-owners had toiled all night to get the Café Green looking its best again. Because the guy really could sing he was forgiven, and invited to a garden fête organised to raise money for Clacton Hospital. Here, Mrs. Smith's clever monkey scratched about and raised £2.50.

St Christopher's Church

The estate was taking shape when a little bit of heaven came along in July 1932. Suntanned people were dressed casually for its first church service, after the Bishop of Chelmsford had said 'they can wear beach pyjamas if they wish!' After hearing about the 'Big City' growing up near Clacton, he decided a service in the area might be a good idea. In fact the Freeholders' committee had already contacted the Rev. H.G. Redgrave of St James's Church, Clacton, with this idea in mind.

The Rev. Redgrave conducted the service, bringing with him his own pianist to play a series of rousing hymns in a huge marquee. Sun-worshippers lying on the sand, hearing the music, must have thought they had died and gone to heaven, or had had too much sun; some headed off in the direction of the singing and joined in.

That evening the marquee was used to hold a concert, the first ever put on by the Freeholders' entertainment committee. Acts included 'Alleged Comedian "Julius" and Frederick Yeomans', the latter a well-known baritone of the day who often sang in the Albert Hall. Although admission was free a collection was made during the service for the church fund.

Stedman donated the site of the church to the Freeholders, and started their collection with a cheque for £50. The Freeholders named the little church, lovely in its simplicity, St Christopher's. On one door it has a plaque showing St Christopher carrying a child over water. It cost £900 to build, seats 250 and was dedicated on 1 July 1933. Holiday-makers and the Stedman family attended. Messrs. H.C. Walker and G.H. Webster were churchwardens for the day. Dressed in white flannels and navy blazers, they welcomed the bishop on his arrival to conduct the service.

The good times got better; it was the age of dance bands, Frank Sinatra, Perry Como and of course, Bing Crosby. The frenetic charleston had given way to the modern waltz. When the latest castophone sound system was set up on the green, Stedman, who was by now referred to as their 'King' or 'Fairy God-father', danced and jigged about. 'The Children of Jaywick', drawing a circle around him, encouraged him but Mrs. Stedman, who was working on the stalls as well as helping to run various competitions, sniffed the air and allowed her slightly tipsy husband to go solo.

A CHURCH OF ENGLAND

Service

will be held for the first time at Jaywick

on

SUNDAY, JULY 31st, 1932

conducted by the

Rev. H. G. REDGRAVE,
Vicar of St. James, Clacton.

The Service will be held in the Marquee at 6 p.m., and you are cordially invited to attend and help to make it a success.

————

Jaywick Sands Freeholders' Association.

51 A Freeholders' handbill advertising the first Church of England service, August Bank Holiday 1932.

52 Frank Stedman (second left) seen here in 1934 talking to Mr. and Mrs. H.C. Walker (Mr. Walker was Honorary Secretary and Treasurer of the Freeholders and a church official), and Mr. and Mrs. P. Marsh. On the extreme left is Mr. G.H. Peters.

53 St Christopher's Church, which opened in 1933.

5

The Happiest Resort on the Essex Coast

The estate was hailed by the press and the people as a remarkable achievement . An extract from the *Daily Chronicle* of 9 August 1929 read:

> At the Southern end of Clacton there are acres and acres of wide flat meadows where the grass grows strong and the larks and yellow hammers sing at all hours of the day. There too you can become a land owner very cheaply. For £50 you can acquire the freehold of 1,000 square feet with a hut upon it coloured so gaily that you would feel as if you were living in a revue ... here it seems like the land of continual summer. You can catch the sound of the sea from beyond the wall. To have the stir of the cool wind at the sea's edge and the snug inland peace of meadows only a step further away, seems the very luxury of a holiday climate.

Stedman's sales brochures read:

> Not many years ago it was impossible to buy at low cost a seaside cottage just for the weekend and holiday use. Since the arrival of Jaywick this is fortunately no longer the case, for here it has been found possible to provide all the essentials at a cost which families of moderate and even small income can easily afford. There are only two seaside places within easy motoring distance of North and East London. Southend is one of them; the alternative is Clacton; a run of 60 miles easily done between late breakfast and lunchtime.

Jaywick Sands became known as 'one of the happiest resorts on the Essex Coast'. 'If it's a crime to be happy there must be more criminals there than anywhere else in the country',

54 Sample property, 1930.

35

55 The first estate office, Beach Road, looking towards Golf Green Road in 1932.

56 The second estate office, seen here in 1934, was situated at The Close, Old Town.

57 Stedman's sales office on Beach Road, seen here on the extreme right, in the 1960s.

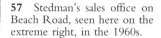

remarked the Freeholders' solicitor Mr. Hodge at the opening of the miniature railway. 'They're just like one big happy family with the Stedmans as their parents', commented Miss Bowman, Gala Chairman and councillor for Finsbury, at another event.

The news was out and people rushed to the farm by the sea. The demand for property increased even though water was being sold for 1d. a pail because there was no supply obtainable through the taps beyond Brooklands Gardens.

Stedman put a stop to this whilst keeping abreast of it all. Delighted with the result of 'The Jaywick Decision', he turned his estate office on Beach Road into a holiday bureau managed by his son, Reginald. A main estate office was built at The Close in The Village in 1934.

'Foff's Corner', Stedman's own holiday home, was erected on the corner of the golf links. Facing the sea, the panoramic views and changing skies inspired many of his paintings.

There were often beach parties where food was eaten on long sticks round blazing fires built with wood collected on the beach during the day. Rashers played giddy tunes, kettles whistled, and under the stars, whooping and twirling, flushed dancers jigged until night turned to day.

Stedman, who could be great fun, had no problem making friends. His circle included Councillor A. Quick who established the *Clacton Times* (the firm of Messrs. A. Quick and Co. Ltd. built up an extensive printing business in Clacton), several other councillors and Mr. G. Lansbury M.P.

Mrs. Stedman, whose family was her life-blood, smiled when Stedman said he was buying a home for their retirement. She recalled that back in 1916 Stedman had bought a cottage in Kent on 10 acres for £2,500 for 'their old age', only to sell it soon after to finance his career as a developer. But her generous husband, who got rid of money as fast as he made it and often gave away strips of land, was sure this time. 'West Lodge', a mock-Tudor house, was built on West Road, Clacton, and became their permanent home in the late 1940s.

Brooklands Club

The marquee was sadly missed and Jack Stedman, who was 'into everything' and is believed to have encouraged his father to go into beach huts and chalets, felt the plot-owners could do with their own place to meet. A generous man like his father, he offered them a loan of £100 to get them started.

Within weeks a building was erected at the back of the Beach Café at a cost of £300. Increasing membership meant that another building had been erected around the original by 1934. This became Brooklands Social Club. The chairman, Mr. Hobbs, was clearly anxious to make it a success. The local paper, the *Times and Gazette*, reported on Mr. Hobbs and his ideas for the club on 25 August 1934:

> the object of the club is to raise money to improve the estate, especially from a health point of view, he therefore hoped, they would rally round and make it a success so that Jaywick could be a place fit to live in. He hoped the accommodation [it cost £3,000 to renovate and contained a hall 110ft. by 90ft., a stage, dressing rooms and a fully licensed bar, completed in only three months] would allow a constant extension. The Social Club Committee would have a hard task running the Club from the point of view of expense and organisation, but given the proper support he was certain their task would be successful.

The club was a success. Membership was five shillings per annum. It opened on a magical Saturday night decorated with hundreds of fairy lights, and floodlit by the Colchester Corporation. Everything was beautifully done; people wore paper hats and party clothes. It was like 'Christmas in July'.

They sang at the top of their voices 'I belong to Jaywick' to the tune of 'I belong to Glasgow', and stamped and clapped their approval when Jack stepped up to open the club officially.

On 25 August 1934, at Foff's Corner, Stedman gave a local reporter his views on the estate:

> Such a scheme has not been carried out without difficulties, sheer obstinacy got me through, having set myself the task, I carried it out.
> Starting with just 12 bungalows, most of these early settlers are still in Jaywick, who often said they thought they had found a kind of Robinson Crusoe island, where they could be quiet and peaceful and

58 *Above.* Frank Stedman teeing off near Foff's Corner in 1935.

59 Mr. and Mrs. Stedman in the garden of their retirement home, West Lodge, in the 1950s.

60 West Lodge, West Clacton, in 1994.

enjoy the difficulties of going to the farmhouse for the well water. But they did not realise the fact that, once started, so many others would find out themselves the healthful air and the advantages of the district. The importance of Jaywick to Clacton is not often realised as completely as it might be. The estate is to be developed in town planning lines, and not the casual efforts of 'Jerry builders'. Jaywick contributes a large amount of money to the rates of Clacton, and the people pay the same rates in the pound as Clacton people. Without the will of the people I should have been powerless to do what I have done.

The public demand for this type of thing cannot be stifled, but can be controlled and guided as it has been.

The Freeholders' entertainment committee, experts at organising fund-raising events, hit the jackpot with their three-day Gala in August 1934. This raised £400 for the Essex Fund for the Blind. The sun burned through clothes, sea spray settled on lips, and people clutched 6d. tickets hoping to win the freehold bungalow on Meadow Way which was due to be raffled.

61 An advertisement for the Jaywick Gala Fête, August 1934.

62 The prize bungalow for the Gala Fête, August 1934.

OH YES! OH YES!! OH YES!!!

Freehold Bungalow
TO BE GIVEN AWAY AT

Jaywick Gala Fete
(CLACTON-ON-SEA)

In aid of the

ESSEX FUND FOR THE BLIND

Organised by the National Institute for the Blind, Registered under the Blind Persons Act, 1929)

AUGUST BANK HOLIDAY, TUESDAY & WEDNESDAY, 6th, 7th and 8th AUGUST, 1934.

To be opened at 2.30 each day.   Bank Holiday by:
CAPT. SIR BEACHCROFT TOWSE, V.C., K.C.V.O., C.B.E.
Tuesday by: **The Rt. Hon. GEORGE LANSBURY, M.P.**
Wednesday by: **SIR JOHN PYBUS, Bart., C.B.E., M.P.**
Chairman: **F. C. STEDMAN, Esq.**

TICKETS ON SALE EVERY DAY

At the Freehold Bungalow, Meadow Way, and at the Jaywick Sands Estate Office   (kindly lent by Messrs. Stedman).

Next Door to the Palace, Clacton-on-Sea.

Also may be obtained from the Blind Tile Maker, on the Café Green.

A 6d. TICKET ADMITS FREE TO GALA.

Hon. Organisers: **The Jaywick Freeholders' Association.**

63   The Gala 'Snow Queen', Gladys Pritchard, being crowned by blind Sir Beachcroft Towse, VC., KCVO., CBE. Frank Stedman is on the left.

Detached and named 'Beachcroft', after Sir Beachcroft Towse, the blind chairman of the association, who had opened the event, the bungalow was tiled by Stan Lawford, a blind tiler who gave up his holiday to work on the bungalow.

Stedman, who had given the site free, did a turn dressed in pyjamas as the 'Lady in The Bed'. The Rt. Hon. George Lansbury M.P., Stedman's house-guest for the week, handed out gifts and prizes and joined the circle of happiness. Sir John Pybus, M.P. for Harwich

1929-35, also Minister of Transport, rode on the roundabout and swings provided by Bert Stokes. It tried to rain, but the sun returned. People enjoyed the sideshows and had fun.

The Gala 'Snow Queen', dressed in sparkling white, was dark-haired Gladys Pritchard of Ealing, who had sold 700 roses, which counted as votes. Five 'White Princesses' brought a 'touch of class to the event'. Smelling salts had to be called for when Mrs. Scaff from Colchester, realising she had won the bungalow, almost passed out.

The Freeholders' Three-Year Plan

In 1936 the Freeholders outlined a three-year framework to enable their committee to space improvements year by year. Every member was written to because it was estimated that to make the scheme work £3 per hut was required over three years. Improvements included:

Preparing for main drains in 1938 (council's plans to sewer the area at a cost of approximately £1,500, it was revealed during this time, would not happen for some years, due to the magnitude of the scheme) purchasing land for a lake and sports, renewing lifebelts and fixing suitable stands, extending lifeboat alarms, getting consent from the Essex Rivers Catchment Board to make Brooklands the first line of defence; when obtained, cut away existing sea wall on Brooklands to give access to all avenues from Midway etc.

Later Stedman was approached about work they felt he should take over. By now working at The Village, he promised them the £1,000 which he would derive annually from this section. (Because of a fire that destroyed records, the Freeholders were unable to confirm if Stedman carried out this promise.)

The Playdrome (a casino and amusement arcade), The Savoy (an amusement centre) and The Tivoli, with floodlit roller skating and free skating instruction, opened at Brooklands along the front. A rock factory opened at Brooklands Gardens (today the community centre) and shops sold souvenir pens, ashtrays, glass paper-weights and 'snowstorms' with a 'Present from Jaywick' written on them.

The Morocco Club

The Morocco Club was owned by pretty Mrs. Elgar who had run the Beach Café and the teahouse in the old farmhouse. It was built on the last site to be sold for business purposes and opened on Beach Road during May 1936. A tall white building with arched windows, it was built along Moorish lines and looked a bit like a Sultan's palace. It had a café in the front and a club at the back and provided darts, billiards and snooker.

64   The Morocco Club was built in 1935. The area outside was used as a Sunday market and can be seen here in the 1960s.

65   A charming bridge in Jaywick Gardens in the 1930s. It was situated to the rear of the Morocco Club in The Village. Sadly it no longer exists.

Known as the 'Nightspot on the Broadway', there was an attractive airy sunlit room above the dancefloor set apart for children—always an important consideration on the estate. A putting green was laid out at the back where crazy golf competitions were held. Players used rubber golf balls, potatoes or cotton reels and competed for prizes of ladies' and gents' watches. A group called 'The Jaywick Follies' played to packed audiences three times a day in The Arcadia which afterwards became The Las Vegas, located directly opposite The Morocco.

The Miniature Railway

The council turned down Stedman's offer of 27 acres free of charge for use as an aerodrome for the area, even though market value was then £200 per acre and the Government was encouraging such ventures. (In 1914 there was a seaplane station at Jaywick.) It did, however, accept his invitation to celebrate the arrival of the miniature railway which opened on Saturday 31 July 1936.

In his article 'A Little known Essex Miniature Railway' (September 1976), Mr. E.F. Morton recorded the popularity of the little train. Reginald Stedman's idea, the train served a practical purpose as well as being a holiday attraction—it connected Jaywick with Crossways which is one mile away.

The Miniature Railways & Specialist Engineering Company of Eastbourne, Sussex, designed and installed the train that was constructed by R.H. Morse and C.F. Parson at Mr. Morse's works in Henfield. The engine, a 19th-century 18" Gauge Live Steam model of a GNR 4-2-2 Sterling 'Single' Locomotive, had been built in 1898 by the students of Regent Street Polytechnic, London, as an engineering exercise. Mr. Notter, Great Northern Locomotive Superintendent at Kings Cross, acquired it and kept it until 1920.

Reginald set the wheels in motion, and after only nine short months the train was ready for its first journey. It was painted Southern green with a cream roof and had three beautifully fitted out carriages with electric lights.

In 1933 Clacton was well established and by 1936 over 100,000 visitors had arrived by train alone. Only hours after the L.N.E.R. decided to spend £180,000 on improving the line between Clacton and Colchester, the Jaywick line was officially opened.

After operating for a week previously in pouring rain, the train rumbled from Jaywick station with Mr. R.T. Johnson of Henfield at the controls. (The regular driver, Mr. R. Bloomfield, earned £2.50 a week for working a 12-hour day, seven days a week.)

Mr. C.H. Newton, Divisional General Manager of the L.N.E.R., opened it and cut the tape using an inscribed pair of gold scissors presented to him by five-year-old Neil, Reginald Stedman's son. Neil, who with two cousins was dressed for the occasion in guard and crew uniforms, was allowed to take charge of the train for a short while.

Mr. J. Carter, Chairman of Clacton Council, and Mr. Lewis, Clerk to the Council, along with several other councillors joined Mr. F. Bryan, traffic manager of the Eastern National Omnibus Company Limited, and several Jaywick residents on the trip.

Running at 35 m.p.h. and pulling a 15-ton load, the train ran down an embankment on a single track, click-clacking along the line. It ran on through a 60-ft. long tunnel before turning across the marshlands, bridging a stream on the way to Crossway station.

Operating twice an hour every day including Sunday, it carried more than 50 passengers at a charge of 6d. for adults, 4d. for children, and 9d. a return regardless of age. It carried up to 2,000 passengers a day all through the summer and was operated by a conductor and driver. The ticket hut, situated on the old sea wall at Jaywick, was seldom used.

At the celebration luncheon in The Morocco, a buoyant Stedman, his blue eyes alive with joy, bounced on to the stage to address the council and Mr. Newton: 'Do you realise your opportunities,' his happy voice boomed, 'you could be a super-Bournemouth because of your geographical position at Clacton—it's up to you'. Referring to the L.N.E.R. as 'our big brother' he joked: 'I heard rumours of a desire for amalgamation with the L.N.E.R.—but we'll not be stampeded into any unwise terms.'

66 & 67 *Right and below.* Mr. Newton at the opening of the Jaywick Miniature Railway. Frank Stedman's grandchildren can be seen wearing miniature guard's uniforms.

68 *Below.* 'Filling up' at Crossways Station in 1936. The sales office can be seen in the background. A close-up of Loco No.1. It was modelled on the 1898 GNR 4-2-2 Sterling 'Single' Locomotive.

The Grand Gala Fête, 1936

The holiday-makers lived it up, the hawthorn bloomed and died, and the train continued to pull its weight around Jaywick. Now that carnival time had come round there was much to do.

After voting in Miss Jaywick, it was decided to enter a decorated float in the shape of a lifeboat named 'Jaywick for Happiness'. A beaming Miss Jaywick arrived back at the estate on the winning float crowned Clacton and District Beauty Queen. Eileen Wallas, from Golf Green Road, dressed in a white gold embroidered dress with an ermine trimmed purple cloak, was flanked by attendants dressed as fairies and garden gnomes. She had spent a strenuous week in Clacton but could now rule over her own subjects for a day as the Freeholders, in conjunction with the Clacton Carnival Committee, had arranged a Carnival Fête and a procession in aid of Clacton Hospital. The procession assembled at Belsize Avenue, New Town, at 11 a.m. for the judging by the queen. With her long hair falling on her shoulders and her eyes shining, she arrived as parade marshals Mr. Ayling, Chairman of the Parks and Sports Committee, and Stedman's sales manager Mr. Johnson rushed about keeping the show on the road.

One car, decorated to look like an earwig, was a favourite with the crowds of onlookers and children especially, but the prize went to 'Tudor Houses' which had been entered by a local builder. The people lined the roads when the entrants proceeded round the estate, cheering and waving them on. Councillor Green conveyed greetings on behalf of the Carnival Committee before Eileen declared the fête open.

69 The 'Jaywick for Happiness' Float, 1936.

70 An auction being held for the Clacton Hospital at a fête in 1936.

This was another great day for the Jaywickians. Sideshows included 'Bucket and Ball', 'Clear the Lines', a spinning wheel, coconut shies, Chinese figure writing and a treasure hunt. They all brought the cash rolling in.

That afternoon a concert was given by Mr. T. Harold and Company from the Theatre. A gymnastic display was put on by the Clacton Christ Church Gymnasium Club. Blindfold boxing and cock-fighting formed part of the entertainment and visitors were invited to take part in competitions arranged by the gymnasts.

'Uncle Peter', who as usual arranged sports for the children, helped with a carnival dance in The Morocco that evening where Mrs. Elgar took charge.

Butlin's

During 1902 Mr. D.C. Preston who came from Dulwich, Stedman's home town, laid out three large housing estates in Little Holland, today Holland-on-Sea, to the east of Clacton.

In 1936 another person with development in mind was establishing himself in the area: Mr. W.E. Butlin or 'King of the Holiday Camps'. He applied in December to build on a 28-acre site at West Road. There was considerable local opposition and the Bishop of Chelmsford urged the council to refuse consent, since even at their best, 'holiday camps were not suitable things to be allowed in the neighbourhood of a girls' school'. However, after several council meetings the application was approved by 12 votes to five.

Councillor Elliott said: 'Butlin would have a great laugh over the council because he had induced them to scrap their by-laws and Town Planning in his favour'. His plan infringed the same by-laws as the Jaywick estate, and ran contrary to the New Town Planning Scheme. Yet Butlin, who treated unconvinced councillors to a visit to his amusement park at Skegness and was willing to spend £70,000 out of his own pocket plus £6,000 in advertising alone, was successful.

After attending the opening of the camp on a sunny afternoon in June 1938, a journalist wrote: 'Billy Butlin has done more for England that St George!'. Stedman, who estimated that his estate now had a summer population of 16,000, watched the developments from his retirement home which he had built opposite the camp long before it was established.

Town Planning

The new Regional Town Planning Scheme prohibited or restricted building in New Town and covered most of Jaywick but excluded Brooklands.

Jaywick as a whole had become an area of dense settlement: there were 29 plots per acre in Brooklands, 20 per acre in The Village and 9 per acre on the Tudor Estate. This high density housing and the cost of providing future social services were sources of concern for the council.

When the Freeholders pointed out that Brooklands was included in their by-laws, and as such was entitled to the same facilities as the rest of the estate, the council suggested that if density could be reduced in that area to 10 dwellings to the acre then other proposals would be considered. The Freeholders complained that this was an almost impossible task, but neverthe-less collaborated with Stedman and took advice on town planning from a specialist in this field.

Court Action, 1936

The association found flooding on the estate one of its biggest and most expensive headaches; it drained its finances time and time again. When it occurred in January 1936 in the Tendring Section on land belonging to Stedman's daugh-ters, it was so bad that it prevented access to bungalows. Letters of protest were sent to the Essex Rivers Catchment Board and the Ministry of Health, but replies were not received.

Jaywick was forced to take matters into its own hands and Mr. Hobbs, Chairman of the Freeholders, instructed workmen to cut a hole in the sea wall and release the water; the situation improved. However, workmen from the Board then arrived and filled in the opening, and the whole area flooded again. This led to Jaywick Property Ltd. and a representative plot-owner, Mr. Symes from London, issuing a lawsuit blaming the Board for the flooding.

During a ten-day hearing it was learned that Stedman had previously had to repair cuts he made in the sea wall after a member of the Board, Mr. Hutley, complained in February 1931. Although Justice Atkinson, who spent several days in Jaywick, ruled in favour of the plot-owners, the Board, claiming it was only doing its statutory duty by keeping the farm-land at the back of the estate free of salt water, appealed successfully to the High Court. Although permission was granted for a further appeal to the House of Lords the plot-owners decided not to go any further, and the Freeholders, who had spent thousands of pounds

on the appeal, instead decided to negotiate with the Board, which would be taking the wall over anyway.

On the Essex coast the North Sea has always reigned supreme. Dressed in a mantle of sunshine it looks beautiful and sparkles like the crown jewels; angry it becomes a spiteful, huge monster, sweeping over and crashing against anything in its path.

In December 1936 the highest tides in 40 years were recorded. The Board spent £5,000 on improvements at Lion Point where the water had come over, and worked on plans for a concrete wall; this plan was held up because of the war. Instead a temporary 13ft. wall was built in front of the Tendring Section at a cost of £2 5s. per annum for owners of bungalows rated at £9. The work was completed in 1937.

In 1938 the council acquired the ancient manorial rights for the shore when it was considering a scheme to extend the promenade in Clacton. At about this time Stedman purchased the foreshore rights (land above high water mark) for £1,500 in order to prevent them falling into the wrong hands. He eventually owned the foreshore from the golf links to the Martello Tower, thus becoming one of the few private beach owners in the whole country. He promised the plot-owners free access to the beach but by now they were wary of Stedman's promises and insisted that this be put in writing. Over the years they came to distrust any kind of authority whatsoever, or any meddling in their affairs.

Improvements continued about the estate. A first-aid hut and life-saving alarms were set up as far as Lion Point, and an application was submitted to the council for a redistribution of its area in order that Jaywick could become a separate ward.

An article that appeared in the local paper in 1933, reproduced in G. Hardwick's *Paper Clips* (Melody Press, Clacton-on-Sea), read:

Guess where all this is taking place. Eastern princes with their harems, mosques and desert scenes, a slave market with traders bidding lovely slaves and Ali Baba and the 40 thieves. Well it's all going on in Clacton Town Hall. So get elected to the council as soon as possible.

71 Sea defence work at Brooklands in 1935.

72 Flooding at Brooklands in December 1936.

Reginald Stedman, having served in the army and spent several years after the war involved in developments at Bognor and Hastings, now lived in Clacton. Perhaps encouraged by the above, he decided to run for election in 1938 but his luck was out and he was unsuccessful. By May 1962 there were two councillors for the newly created Golf Green ward, and six representing the West Ward.

Jaywick and the War

A reader of the *Daily Mirror* in August 1939 asked: 'Why is there no pub in Jaywick?' and signed himself 'Dry'. He warned: 'Take a tip, if you're fond of a pint and go to Jaywick, you're in for a disappointment'.

The reply highlighted the frustration of would-be pub owners in the area: 'Jaywick Sands being a newly developed part of the world is obviously suffering from alcoholic drought because with de-licensing going on steadily all over the country you've as much chance of getting a licence for a new pub these days as you have of selling fur coats to Zulus'.

Brooklands Club and the Farmhouse continued to do well, and new songs such as 'The Lambeth Walk', a hit from the show 'Me and My Girl', became popular. Stedman joined the dancers and two-stepped through the chorus shouting a loud 'Oi!' on the last beat whenever he had the opportunity.

Winter passed, and fragrant primroses, tulips, and daffodils filled gardens and jam-jars: Easter 1939 had arrived and it was glorious. Smiling children abandoned toys and pets to tuck into painted eggs during the hottest Easter on record for 11 years—the estate had 40 hours of sunshine.

All too soon however, grim-faced people heard Prime Minister Neville Chamberlain declare war on Germany on 3 September 1939. Hours before war was officially declared, evacuees were already on the move. Labelled like luggage, clutching a change of clothes in brown paper and with gas masks swinging from their necks, hoards of dejected children set off. On 6 September 250 mothers with children under school age arrived in Clacton. Jack

Stedman and Mr. Johnson were put in charge of billeting in Jaywick. Owners of accommodation on the estate allowed it to be used for evacuation purposes. Although 100 were accommodated initially, there was room for 600 later. Before long children in the district were themselves evacuated to places of safety when buildings were bombed.

Stedman's baby had become a restricted area; Billy's chest pains and Jimmy's nightmares were now left in the care of the people along the Essex coast, who for many years had catered to thousands. Those with no business in the area needed permits to get in. Army personnel replaced holiday-makers, and the need for scrap iron metal forced the lifting of the railway track. The train that had brought so much joy was dismantled, stock was stored and the surroundings were rapidly requisitioned for coastal defence.

In their excellent book on plotland development, *Arcadia for All*, Dennis Hardy and Colin Ward wrote about plotland development on the east and south coast, recording that during the war Jaywick became part of a national coastal survey. Civil servant Mr. P.J.F. Mansfield's comments on Jaywick in a ministerial memorandum were interesting, but lacked favour with some of the residents, who at that time had no inkling they were being watched:

I found this extraordinary piece of holiday shack development surprising and rather interesting in a way, though it does leave one perhaps with a feeling of some nausea about it all. There are many hundreds of wooden shacks erected without proper regard for the right use of materials or proper layout but it is an inescapable fact that the colony does provide for many thousands of holiday-makers each year to enjoy a holiday by the sea, under living conditions of some independence.

The Jaywick Estate, though it is emphatically not a piece of development that should ever have been allowed to grow up in its present form, is there, and must be accepted, as it does provide admirable holiday facilities for great numbers each year. But there must be greater control of all future developments both in the design of the huts and the layout of the land. Extensive developments here would be quite justified and would, incidentally, possibly be the means of saving other areas elsewhere from speculation, and this is not unimportant as the Coast has not so much left unspoilt that the good areas can be encroached upon with impunity.

6

The Winds of Change

War came to an end on 8 May 1945, seven days after May Day. In bygone days people went out on this day at dawn to welcome the advent of spring. Now people poured into the streets to celebrate the end of the war. Wearing home-made paper hats with 'V-for-Victory' signs glued to the front, servicemen clambered up lamp posts, motorists sounded thousands of horns and people cried with sheer joy.

Owners returned to Jaywick glad to be alive and free. The grim days of war were not forgotten but put to the back of the mind. There were tears and prayers for fun-loving Jack Stedman, killed in the war, but work needed to be tackled. The narrow avenues had been torn apart, and barbed wire still protected the sandy beaches.

The Freeholders applied for a war damage settlement. The War Department at first refused to acknowledge any financial liability and just offered £2,000 but by 1950 this had risen to approximately £31,500, a sum that paid a great deal of bills.

In the early part of this century holidays with pay were comparatively unknown; those who did manage a break from work usually had one week only. Due to the Holiday with Pay Act of 1938, delayed until after the war, people throughout the country had more money to spend. Many who had had to scrimp and save during the war let their hair down and enjoyed themselves; Jaywick Sands buzzed.

The shops did record business. Hammering went on most weekends and before long repainted homes and tidied-up gardens looked brighter. Housewives dusting and cleaning utility furniture and dishes, hummed and sang the wartime rhyme:

> Because of the pail, the scraps were saved,
> Because of the scraps, the pigs were saved,
> Because of the pigs, the rations were saved,
> Because of the rations, the ships were saved,
> Because of the ships, the island was saved,
> And all because of a housewife's pail.

Jaywick was more popular after the war although throughout the late 1940s and '50s the first signs of the decline in seaside holidays were apparent. People were opting more and more for holidays abroad.

73 Holiday-makers promenading in the 1940s.

74 Brooklands race track, 1935.

The nation celebrated the marriage of Princess Elizabeth to Prince Philip of Greece. At Buckingham Palace a series of glittering parties took place—at one Princess Julian of the Netherlands slipped to the floor and had to be hauled up.

There was no slipping up when Mrs. Elgar set her cap at Stedman's sales manager. The plot-owners sensed 'love was in the air', and celebrated the wedding of the fiery redhead. The reception was held in The Morocco, which was later rented out when the bride and groom decided to move on.

Sport was always popular in Jaywick and a favourite one was hare racing, with events such as the Colchester Stakes and the Jaywick Stakes. A miniature racing track near Snakes Lane opened. Managed by 'Curly', a jolly Irishman, it became a favourite with children. He would pay a couple of pence to those who ran out onto the track to flag excited winners down.

A greyhound track operated at the back of Meadow Way and a go-kart track operated at Brooklands for a time. The Freeholders built a model boating lake on the Café Green, with benches round it where people could relax and watch. Young children loved to splash about or sail paper boats, painstakingly made out of newspaper by their fathers.

The Jaywick & Tudor Ratepayers

Completion of the Tudor Estate was slowed down because of the consequences of the war, the new building regulations, and the dreadful 1947 winter when the sea froze over. Mr. Reginald Howard, an independent local builder, built the first house on the section.

After the war many families who had been bombed out of East London moved permanently to their home by the sea. Few could afford cars or telephones, but they were willing to put up with the poor quality roads and the inadequate lighting at nights as well as the sharp winter winds, in order to live in Jaywick.

The Freeholders, who since the early days had shown exceptional energy, had some responsibility lifted from their shoulders by the formation of a new association called 'The Jaywick Ratepayers'. They changed the name later to the 'The Jaywick & Tudor Ratepayers'. Starting with 156 members, from December 1950 this association took responsibility for The Village and the Tudor Estate. I shall refer to The Jaywick & Tudor Ratepayers as the Ratepayers throughout this book.

They wanted better roads, bus shelters, a public hall and a resident doctor as the estate by now had a large number of elderly residents. On learning that there was no chance of getting

£144,000 for roads due to the state of finance throughout the country, they set out on a 'Self Help' improvement scheme started by Frank and Dennis Allum with £10. £100 was donated by Stedman to aid the fund.

When they approached the council and asked it to take over the town-planned section of the estate, councillors who welcomed what they called 'this live association', although sympathetic, pointed out that some adopted roads in Clacton were considered worse than those in Jaywick— all roads had to be made up to an acceptable standard before they could be adopted and maintained by the authorities. The council did have powers to make temporary repairs to roads, and the associations urged them to interpret these liberally and to spend up to the limit of £10 at Jaywick from time to time. Councillor Quick said: 'Councillors were leaning over backwards to further the interest of Jaywick, but it would not become "a garden city overnight", even if legal and other matters could be sorted out.'

There was always another major problem with the roads on the estate; there was still no one who could prevent drivers of vehicles damaging them. Stedman was approached about the matter by Mr. P. Holmes, Chairman of the new association, who 'prayed the day would come when council took over the roads'. He also suggested erecting a memorial to Stedman for developing 'one of the most unique holiday towns in the British Isles'. This was a minority view however, for many were heartily sick of forking out rates, membership fees, and so on when all they really wanted was a carefree holiday. Upset that the promise of 'main drainage and good concrete roads' had not been kept by Stedman, they decided that 'he should be shot!'.

Holmes reported to members that Stedman said he had no further interest in the estate except for land the crown would not let him do anything with. (Mr. Neil Stedman insisted that his grandfather never lost interest in Jaywick.)

Stedman agreed at this January 1952 meeting to enforce covenants people had entered into and to prohibit parking on grass verges, but he refused responsibility for anything else. When Councillor Ball, a guest speaker at a meeting on 6 October 1950, addressed members he commented that:

> surface water drainage on the estate did not form part of the council's sewage. No plans were ever deposited showing the whereabouts of the gullies and so on. Those surface water drains that did exist had outfalls into open ditches or fleets and council was under no obligation, and had no right to interfere with these in any way. Those taken over under a 1934 agreement with Stedman were taken over as foul sewers only. Jaywick people should get a fair run for their rates, and were right to seek the same amenities as were enjoyed by other ratepayers, but the matter rested with the Ministry and the council. It was hoped, because work at Jaywick was urgent, the Ministry would treat the matter a little bit out of the ordinary.

Relations between the council and Jaywick were strained from the beginning, but efforts were made throughout the years by both sides to build bridges. Socially they got on well; Jaywick was only across a board table that their disagreements were evident. The remarks made by Councillor N.W. Hardgrave, guest of honour at an annual dinner-dance held in *The Glengariff*, Clacton, were greeted with prolonged and mounting applause:

> It has been said council is not interested in Jaywick— take my word for it, this is not true. Jaywick takes up a great deal of our time, but the matter will not be solved until Jaywick has an equal place—and with the rest of council—is one community. Then you will realise you are not an unwanted orphan and you will be an adopted child. With association members co-opted on to the council there will be closer co-operation.

Clacton had problems of its own to cope with at this time. Two of its largest hotels had closed down, reflecting a trend throughout the county in which many were being turned into apartment buildings.

Bucket and spade holidays were going out of fashion. People's tastes were becoming more sophisticated and self-catering holidays and holidays abroad were more popular. Butlin's felt the 'winds of change', and now had to compete with Pontin's and Warner's. By 1964 Mr. Butlin, hoping to boost holiday trade, offered £1,000 per annum for five years to the publicity departments in Ayr, Bognor, Filey, Minehead, Barry, Skegness and Pwllheli, as well as the use of his own publicity department. He believed resorts in England had more to offer than their foreign competitors and were more pleasant despite bad weather.

Flooding in Jaywick

The south-east coast of England has frequently suffered flooding, with records dating as far back as 1790. The significant factor is that each flood has been progressively higher than its predecessor.

At the end of the 19th century the *Essex Naturalist* reported that the great flood in 1897 'would be long remembered'. The floods on 6-7 January 1928 were described as 'the highest flood-tide within living memory'.

In 1906, in an attempt to explain the continuing height of flood-tides in Essex a Royal Commission on Coastal Erosion and Reclamation of Tidal Lands, published a report stating:

> It is believed that either the coastline of this part of Essex is gradually sinking, or that from some unknown cause the tides are higher than formerly the case. At present the theory suggested to explain the sinking of south-east England is that northern England and Scotland are recovering from the ice which covered them in the Quaternary Period, and are slowly rising again. In addition, melting ice caps are releasing more water into the sea, thus raising mean sea level.

Spring tides occur between September and April. North Sea surges last only a few hours. Because of gradual subsidence and floods, owners of coastal areas have been forced to build barriers around their property in order to protect it from the tides. This battle to prevent the sea invading the flat low-lying land began when the Romans built simple earth embankments nearly 2,000 years ago to form the first sea defences. New walls were later built, and placed in front of existing walls. These were known as 'counterwalls', and one such is that behind Brooklands.

In 1880 a local Act constituted the Sea Defence Commission with powers to provide protective works for the whole of the cliffs within the Clacton Drainage District. To meet its expenses a rate was to be levied in this area. Later, after a further Act of Parliament was obtained, it was able to collect a reduced rate from the remainder of the parish. In 1905 the commission tried to obtain legislation which would enable it to undertake further improvements, but the council resisted its efforts and obtained a transfer of its powers. Ever since that date it has maintained, improved and extended the protection works in its corner of the Essex coast. When the Coast Protection Act was passed in 1949, this authorised subsidies for that purpose. With the help of Government compensation and voluntary subscriptions the Freeholders spent £22,000 on a sea wall along Brooklands front.

The holiday season usually ended by mid-October. Tanned and relaxed, people dragged heavy suitcases home together with sloes, blackberries and elderberries which had been gathered for home-made wines and jams.

Getting through the winter was made easier with lots of hot meat stews, filled with dumplings and herbs. The April showers soon passed and summer salads, swimsuits and sunshine were back in fashion again. Children squealed with excitement; they loved ice-cream, buckets and spades, the sun and the sea, but most of all the donkey rides. 'Lucy', 'Churchill' and 'Daisy' were just three out of a total of 22 donkeys owned by Nora Cleghorn who worked three different pitches at Clacton, Jaywick and St Osyth. At night they were kept on rented land in a field at the back of Meadow Way, The Village, where residents often complained about their braying.

For 45 years Nora operated the pitches, having helped to run the concern with the previous owner, Mr. J. Baden Powell. Up to his death he had owned two donkey stands and a cockle and whelk stall on the west promenade, and was the only man to hold a licence to operate two landaus from 1948. Nora charged 6d. in the early days. To get 'the donks', as she fondly called them, onto the beach she used helpers who would hop on their bikes and herd them through the town. Thriving on all the fuss and attention, the donkeys would saunter along, their shaggy coats spruced up for the season, often holding up the heavy holiday traffic in Jaywick Lane.

Holiday-makers dozed in deck-chairs that first weekend in August 1948. The council had 5,000 deck-chairs ready for hire, and over 1,500 had booked in at Butlin's; it was a bumper holiday weekend. But the North Sea had evil plans: on 8 August, only a week later, storms ripped through Jaywick, almost tearing the little resort apart.

75 Residents at Brooklands after the August 1948 floods.

Boatmen sailed up and down flooded avenues bringing children and elderly people to safety. Red Cross nurses in sea-boots stood by while mattresses, chairs, cushions and suitcases floated along. Children wept and young mums wearing 'New Look' frocks held up with string headed home, their well-earned holiday ruined.

About 2,000 people had to be evacuated and a special train was laid on by the station master at Clacton to get them away. Many wore pyjamas under their coats and borrowed shoes on their feet. About 300 remained and helped mop up the damage, which was estimated at £100,000.

According to a former member of the council of management of the Freeholders, Brooklands resembled the scene of an earthquake. Bungalows leaned in all directions, several beyond repair. Roads were a nightmare to negotiate. There were great lumps of concrete standing at crazy angles, yet holiday-makers still turned up prepared to carry drinking water all the way from the bus stop to put their homes in order.

The same year witnessed a bumper black-berry harvest, and heavy crops were gathered from bushes all over the area and taken to London by lorry to be sold at Covent Garden within hours of being picked.

In 1949, during March, a 70 m.p.h. gale hurled through Jaywick followed by another in October; nothing was spared. The sea crashed over and washed away the Freeholders' wall which had been built from brushwood and clay in front of Brooklands.

Four hundred members in Brooklands and 400 in the other sections were asked for further

76   Outhouses at Grasslands were flooded in the 1948 floods.

77   Flooding in The Village in 1948.

financial assistance to get another wall built. With few pennies in their pockets and fed up with paying out, they dragged their feet.

The first hundred yards of a new concrete wall had already been constructed between November 1949 and February 1950, and the Freeholders decided to call a special meeting for 17 April 1950 to try to resolve the situation.

There had been unrest among members for some time. It was felt that the council of management, in office for 18 years, was slipping. These feelings erupted at this angry meeting when a motion of no confidence in the management committee before 1949 was carried. Several of the old committee, including Chairman Headworth, resigned. Mr. A. Wolfe, former chairman of the Sea Defence Committee, who had owned a bungalow in Brooklands since 1932, became the association's new chairman.

Mr. E. Lansbury, nephew of Mr. G. Lansbury M.P., resigned from the Sea Defence Committee at this time, as did Mr. H. Asbury, another long-time official. Mrs. Anne Wolfe became its new chairman.

When our grandparents sat in carts holding their donkeys in terror of steam-rollers, those were the days of men whose like will never be seen again. Mr. Wolfe, who loved Jaywick, was one of them. A skilled artist, he appreciated everything about the estate. The sea always fascinated him, but he would warn: 'Never underestimate the powers of water; the sea takes no prisoners'. He simply refused to take no for an answer unless he had to, and virtually single-handedly took charge of the situation: it had been his constant criticism that produced the concrete construction in place of the proposed repair to the damaged brushwood and clay wall that had been considered at an emergency meeting in October. He had tremendous organising ability and enthusiasm. Confident that it could be achieved, he had promised members he would get that wall up by the end of the year.

At his first AGM in 1949 the members were brought up-to-date with the financial position and all the efforts which had been made to raise the necessary cash before and since he was elected. £900 alone had been raised in donations; £25 and £50 bond issues bearing three per cent interest repayable in 20 years had raised a further £7,425; but they were still £3,000 short.

The work that he intended was of a more permanent nature than that which had gone before. Wolfe hammered the message home:

78 'Adrian's Wall' was Jaywick's first concrete sea defence. It was known locally after the Freeholder's chairman, Mr. A.A. Wolfe, who had it built in 1950.

they had to get that wall up. Fired by his enthusiasm, impressed members came up with the money. £12,000 was raised, which with loans amounted to £25,500. When this was added to £31,500, part of the war damage settlement agreed by the Treasury, there was enough to pay Messrs. Reed & Mallik of Station Road, Clacton, to finish the 2,100ft. wall.

Forty-five men, including 20 discharged Polish soldiers, completed the whole of Brooklands front at a total cost of £50,000. Included in the cost were a Tarmac promenade and three concrete stairways; work finished on the last day of 1950.

Mr. Wolfe had kept his word and 'Adrian's Wall'—as the wall was named locally—was officially opened on 18 May 1951 by Sir Stanley Holmes, M.P. for Harwich. He cut the tape stretched across the road at Brooklands, watched by more than 200 people. They could sleep better now, secure in the knowledge that this wall, the first concrete sea barrier ever built to protect Jaywick, stood between them and their greatest enemy, the North Sea.

Afterwards Wolfe, who ran his own mosaic business and lived in Chelsea, was presented with a book with a picture of Brooklands on the cover signed by 70 grateful members. A plaque was put on the wall at Brooklands to commemorate the occasion, although this was soured somewhat by the £50,000 sea defence provided for Butlin's at the expense of the taxpayer.

Eight years later Mr. Wolfe reported the clearance of colossal debts, including the contractor's bill and the clearance of £7,775 debentures raised for completing the wall. Meanwhile prices were rising all the time and to keep in front at their AGM the following year the Freeholders increased their charges to £6. The sum per bungalow was for services such as Elsan clearance, road repairs, sea defences, maintenance of the new sea wall, maintenance of equipment and vehicles, and was also to include membership of the association and club.

There was great fun that night. After a three-hour ordeal chairing the meeting, Mr. Wolfe tried to make a point and swung his hammer high; his first deft pass shattered his glass of water, while the second broke the hammer itself as he hit the table. Astonished and red-faced the chairman stared at the offending object as if it had hit him, then pulled himself together and demanded order. This took some time!

At election time personalities themselves sometimes came under the hammer. Mr. Hurdle, an ex-committee member, said that the reason he had ceased to be a member was that differences of opinion were signs of vitality and enlightenment, but the chairman and his wife did not allow this. He had been vilified to a great degree because he would not be 'a yes man', and refused to be encompassed in a 'Hitlerite' strait-jacket.

Mr. Rowlem retorted that in the past he felt there had been 'a secret society who had done what they liked and who were trying to creep back into the council. You will never have another man like Mr. Wolfe, he astonishes me, I only wish he was Prime Minister'.

The Board had raised the wall in The Village section another one to two feet above the high-tide level after the floods of 12-13 February 1938, and then heightened it again in 1944 after more floods, raising it a further 18 inches to two feet above the flood levels of 1949. Now considering Jaywick particularly vulnerable in the event of a breakthrough, during December 1949 detailed emergency plans were formulated to deal with further floods.

The Freeholders appreciated loyalty, but almost blew a fuse after a caring club steward decided to test the reactions of his assistants by organising a 'hold up' when they were taking spirits and the day's takings of £130 from Brooklands Club to the Farmhouse, now back in their possession. It was a hot August night, nearing midnight, when a soft voice said 'stick 'em up!' But the frightened stewards did no such thing—they bolted.

PC Mitchell, the estate's only bobby, a Welshman who everybody agreed resembled film star Errol Flynn, saw the barrow and other objects left across the road by the steward and arrested him. Although the steward said he only did it for a joke and apologised, he was fined £10 at Clacton's Magistrates' Court.

7

The 1953 Floods

The first month of the New Year was almost over when those who switched on their radio for the midnight weather forecast on 31 January 1953 heard the BBC announce, 'it will be cold'. What followed was the greatest peacetime tragedy in the county's history, a night of sheer horror never forgotten by those who survived it. It was Saturday, the night of the full Spring tide, and by 6.15 p.m. there was already a fierce howling gale. It had been cold all day and a surge was known to be on its way from the north, but it was believed this would die away before reaching Essex.

On Thursday 29 January (St Thomas' Day) there had been a major depression near Iceland and subsequent record-breaking winds of hurricane strength over the Orkneys. Storms in the Irish Sea were so bad that the British Rail ferry *Princess Victoria* had sunk on its way to Ireland. The deep atmospheric low over the North Sea had been drawing water into the area. Northerly gales drove a wall of water down the coast; as it funnelled into the narrower areas of the North Sea between England and Holland, this wall of water grew taller. At its peak the surge was 16ft. high.

The English Channel acts as a safety-valve for pent-up water in the southern part of the North Sea. The average movement in the Channel is normally ingoing, that is towards the north-east. But from noon that Saturday the water flowed towards the south-west. It was estimated that on the following Sunday the current was almost eight times stronger than the normal inflow, with an average speed in the Channel of three feet per second. It was a

week later before the water-movement in the Channel returned to normal.

'The great surge', as it was called, the worst storm since 1702, caused damage along a 200-mile stretch of coastland from the Thames to Yorkshire. The oldest section of the wall at Jaywick was in poor condition; years of buffeting by the North Sea had not only damaged the wall but also eroded the sand and shingle beaches that provided some protection. Shifting shingle was worn away, exposing the wall's toe-piles and lowering the beach level. This meant increased wave energy crashing against and over the wall.

The first reports of flooding came at 9 p.m. when the Lincolnshire police announced that there had been widespread flooding between Cleethorpes and Skegness. The harbour-master at Harwich noted that the predicted high-tide level had been reached 3½ hours early. He sent out an alarm message between 10 and 11 p.m. which warned that the entire Essex coast was threatened by the abnormally high tide.

In Jaywick residents went about their business as normal. Mr. H.G. Marshall, who had worked for 20 years for the Board and was keeper of the sluice gates at Holland Haven, noted with increasing alarm the goings on in the angry sea and took the precaution of setting the alarm bell on his machine which recorded the levels of the tide. He set the alarm to sound if a height of 10ft. 4ins. was reached.

Shortly before 10.30 p.m. the alarm bell sounded and at 11.30 p.m. he alerted his engineer at St Osyth that the tide had jumped

3ft. 2ins. in 20 minutes. At 11.15 p.m. word was sent out that Jaywick be warned. The warning was not received until just before midnight, from which point on the plot-owners fought for their lives.

By 1.45 a.m. on Sunday morning there were 22 breaches in the sea wall between Beacon Hill and Colne Point, and a torrent of water was heading east across the St Osyth marshes. The wall at St Osyth was topped. At Lee Wick, Point Clear, about three miles from Jaywick, work was in progress on the sea wall. Because the unhardened clay was not firm enough to withstand the surge, it breached. Long lengths of the wall west of Cocket Wick Farm, at the rear of the estate, were destroyed and large areas were inundated. The lie of the ground channelled the water towards the back of Jaywick, where no danger had been anticipated. As it advanced its speed was increased by the harsh driving wind, and its volume was reinforced by water flowing in from 30 breaches along the St Osyth beach. The water stripped the grass off the marshland on its headlong journey to the 'happiest resort on the Essex Coast'. Hit from the side it stood no chance, and was swamped with over 2,000 million gallons of water, which in some places lay six feet deep. Some said it took only seven minutes to flood Jaywick, others reckoned 15; everybody agreed it was swift, cold and cruel.

The tossing, thundering waves roared over the estate. Those who could leapt from their beds to battle with the seething raging water, clinging where, and to whatever they could for safety. Some escaped from the first rush of water onto higher ground or to nearby houses also on higher ground, while others trembling with fear climbed up narrow wooden staircases, so steep they were more like ladders, into attics and onto roofs. They climbed up on top of kitchen tables and draining boards, praying as never before that the invading water creeping up the wall towards them would go no further. They made holes in their roofs so that they could wave to the outside world in a desperate attempt to attract attention. In most cases hours passed before there was an answering signal from a rescue boat.

There were few actual tears, it was claimed, but hysterical calls and screams for help echoed throughout the estate. For years afterwards people were haunted day and night by the sound, while others could not bear to speak about the cries, especially those from petrified animals.

PC Mitchell (Mitch) lived in Jaywick. He saw a caravan rocking its way towards him on a six-foot wave, and knew that this was something more than mere flooding. When Police Sergeant Saville from Clacton arrived to see him on another matter, together they drove to Lion Point to assess the situation.

Although the associations had worked wonders, on that awful night miracles were what was needed. Poor communications were a hindrance to swift action, but nevertheless within minutes a rescue operation was mounted in The Village.

Mr. S.A. Smith, a Jaywick businessman and former magician, had three pleasure boats (dinghies) stored at the Morocco Club for the winter. Although one was out of action, the other two were hauled out and pulled across Beach Road. From here Jim Shepherd, a former Clacton footballer who was Smith's boatman, set off on a rescue mission. He and Smith worked for three days and nights with only two hours of rest during that time.

Inspector S. Barnicoat was on his way to Jaywick when he had to abandon a brand new police car to escape a huge wave. Along with him was PC Joe Burgess who headed for a house with a light on to alert them of the danger. On the way he grabbed a man lying head down in the water and pulled him to safety. PC Donald Harmer also accompanied Barnicoat. It was suggested he should try to get word to Clacton because the line had gone dead when the inspector had tried to make contact.

Meanwhile Smith and Shepherd, who were the only two people able to handle a boat in such conditions, had set off. One rowed the dinghy while the other steadied it and assisted the mostly elderly people into it. On their return the second boat was pushed out and the full one pulled in by a handful of helpers gathered outside The Morocco, the only dry ground in Jaywick.

79 Jim Shepherd (standing), a former Clacton footballer and Mr. Smith's skipper in the 1953 floods. He is seen here collecting 2s. 6d. from his passengers for the half-hour trip along the coast to surrounding areas. The boat named *Tony* was used in the floods and years later sank at sea.

80 Mr. Sidney Smith, a former magician, and his wife Vera. During the 1953 floods, and with the help of his skipper Jim Shepherd, he rescued 30 people using two of his own pleasure boats. Vera, who ran a newsagent's in St Osyth for over twenty years, gave their daughter's clothing to a local policeman and his wife who had lost everything in the floods.

Between journeys mugs of tea laced with brandy brought back from holidays abroad were gulped down as cold gusts of wind, reaching over 175 m.p.h., whistled through frozen bodies.

'Adrian's Wall' had not broken; it had stood firm against the waves but had been topped. 'We'll be back for you!' the men shouted at the top of their voices, hoping to be heard over the biting wind. Terrified people hanging by their frozen fingertips to anything they could grip—barbed wire in some cases— kept praying.

V. & G., a butcher's on Beach Road, is today owned by Jeff and Vicky who run the successful concern with help from staff; a flat

above the shop is rented out. On that night the flat was home to Mrs. Elizabeth Allard, the tiny Commandant of the Jaywick Red Cross Detachment, and her husband. Dubbed afterwards 'the little Florence Nightingale of Jaywick', when neighbours called later her husband often joked, 'Florence is out!'. She was woken at 12.30 a.m by a neighbour. After lighting a blazing-red fire she put a kettle on, and with her husband's help turned the flat into a rescue centre. When this was full the Morocco Club on the other side of the road was taken over. Although Mrs. Elgar had as usual closed for winter, the key was soon located.

The moon, which was extra bright that night, lit a shimmering silver path across the raging sea. Then, as if in spite, it clouded over covering the whole estate in pitch darkness. There was no time to think; white-faced, shocked rescuers did what they could.

Mr. Allard joined the Allum Brothers who were busy warning people about the situation. In the course of this they drove a child with whooping cough to Clacton Hospital, together with its grandmother, who had suffered a heart attack, when being taken out of a property through a window.

On their return they found Jaywick Lane blocked. They worked non-stop for 15 hours even though Frank Allum was only just out of hospital—he was still recovering from a compressed fracture of the spine and a broken arm.

Not sure if his own family was dead or alive, he made his way to the police houses on Union Road, Crossways, shouting: 'Get up ... Jaywick is flooded'. He then dashed to Rush Green Road to alert Clacton Fire Station where he cried, 'They're drowning down at Jaywick!'. He did not have to repeat himself.

Among the rescuers was Barnicoat who, although getting on in years, went into the water up to his waist time and again. Mrs. Shepherd, Jim's wife, was so concerned that she waded in herself to look after him. Exhausted, shivering and red-eyed, he had to be helped away, under protest, hours later.

New Town was isolated for hours. Brooklands, facing the front, was protected by 'Adrian's Wall' and although badly flooded it suffered no fatalities. It was eventually reached via St Osyth on boat from the marsh. One of the biggest breaches of the sea wall took place at the site of the Playdrome Casino, where one wave smashed a 30-yard gap through the concrete. In Grasslands sanitary vehicles were tossed about and landed on the edge of the dykes. Huts were tipped over and and came to rest on their sides. This section was also reached across the marsh.

The Ratepayers had made huge strides but there was still no resident doctor or nurse on the estate, nor was there a chemist. The only medical supplies were obtained from the first-aid post on Beach Road, and this had been broken into.

Jaywick has always been a close community, and on that night people worked as one.

The Red Cross in Jaywick was not represented by Mrs. Allard alone; another stalwart was Mrs. Rita Cass. This remarkable 52-year-old waded out to meet the rescue boats and carried people to dry land on her back. 'I served in the Red Cross in the Second World War, but have never seen anything like this,' she later told a reporter. Jaywick Sands had never seen anything quite like Mrs. Cass either; its people remember her with gratitude and love.

The scene was by now well illuminated by electricity, but the lights failed at about 2.30 a.m. Work continued by candlelight, and at one stage headlights from a Land Rover were beamed onto the rescue boat's path.

The whole scene was a nightmare. Large and small boats alike were ripped from their moorings and flung into the air as if built from tissue paper. Poles, gates, dead cattle, dunnage and spiked fences were everywhere, hampering the rescue; homes simply disintegrated.

The almighty din threatened to split people's eardrums in two. All the while Smith and Shepherd rescued children, the old and the crippled. People lay dead in their beds; others died in the streets. One hero among many that night was 21-year-old PC Harmer who, chin high in water, made his way to the sea wall, near Foff's Corner. A dark-haired man with soft brown eyes, he had been to Jaywick only once—then only halfway. He travelled along the sea wall by moonlight, with water pounding on the golf course on one side of the path, and the tide still high on the other. He inched his way along the slippery wall, crawling painfully on all fours most of the way—in normal conditions this journey is a quarter of an hour's walk. The water hurled over him with demon-like fury but gradually helpless Jaywick, the flooded golf links and the forbidding Martello Tower were all left behind and he reached welcome Clacton.

Using a phone box, probably the one at Butlin's, he reported at about 3.00 a.m. that: '500 are trapped in Jaywick'. (There were in

81   Police Constable D. Harmer, whose courage inspired this book.

82   The route taken by 21-year-old Harmer as he crawled along to get help. The Martello Tower is about halfway to the telephone kiosk at Butlin's.

fact about 600 residents occupying 250 bungalows that night.) Harmer then returned along the same path to let Jaywick know help was on its way. Mrs. Allard saw him sitting in the entrance of the rescue centre; thinking he was overcome with everything she gave him a cup of tea. She knew the real story later.

Mr. Ted Shepherd, Detective Inspector at Clacton Police Station, directed the rescue and salvage work in the flood area in the absence of the Superintendent who was at Harwich, where Bathside had been badly hit. Shepherd acknowledged that the first information about the disaster had come from Harmer.

Incredibly many people in Clacton knew nothing of what was happening around them until it was announced on the Sunday one o'clock news. However, one very wide-awake citizen had seen Harmer, who had collapsed in the street on his way to his digs later, and had rung the station at Clacton to report that a drunken policeman needed help.

While the exhausted Harmer sipped his tea and hundreds prayed, Clacton swung into action. Jaywick's brave and weary heroes had rescued about thirty people since midnight, with no

communication from the outside world. Now reinforcements had arrived.

Mere facts do not tell a story but local journalists, between giving a helping hand where needed, recorded as much as they could of the distressing tale. As a result the fantastic work of local people, some in uniform but most drawn from all walks of life, has been recorded in print.

Clerk to Clacton Council, Mr. C.B. Hearn opened his office at the Town Hall at about 3.15 a.m. He was unable to contact the welfare official who had recently moved, so he made his own arrangements. Meanwhile St John's Ambulance, the Red Cross, Clacton Police, the Fire Brigade and local organisations of all kinds continued to make their way to the stricken area.

Waves continued to crash and curl over Jaywick. It was still bitterly cold and blowing a gale, and almost the entire population was wearing nightclothes. Spare piles of dry clothes were found and handed in where needed.

'Jimmy The Milk' was a milkman in a million—everybody who knew him agreed. From the time he was 14 years of age, he had worked for one local dairy or another, and the estate was always part of his round. A cheerful, good-looking man, he loved Jaywick and its people.

He rescued a dog called Sally, pulling her from beneath overturned furniture. Moreover, despite the inconvenience of a short leg—the result of an accident—he moved swiftly to help the police compile a list of names and addresses of residents. He was then able to lead them to the areas involved, knowing from extra orders who was in residence that Sunday.

PC Mitchell, who had woken Mr. and Mrs. A. Phillips at Lake Way, The Village, never talked of the events except to say, 'I was lucky enough to wake up an elderly couple before the flood waters arrived'. Missing himself for six hours, he was eventually found safe, having leapt onto a roof where he had been trapped. He was later to join his old mate 'Jimmy the Milk' and together they used a rowing and a motor boat to deliver milk in Jaywick.

When speaking of how he waded in waist-high in water to switch off the electric generator in the sub-station at Crossways, friends joked that he must have been drunk at the time; they certainly made sure he was at the first opportunity when he was off duty.

Mr. E. Smith, a St John's Ambulance-man, weaved his way past bobbing furniture to rescue a family of three and two scared Alsatian dogs. Mr. J. Penington, the manager of the Savoy Theatre, Clacton, brought a lorry-load of boats from St Osyth, together with another member of the company.

Mr. Ellis, Jaywick's postman, was another well-known local character. He used his own rowing boat to rescue Audrey and Derek Frost and their son Michael, after trying unsuccessfully to reach the Lorking family. Mrs. Lorking had fallen through a ceiling but had been yanked to safety by the hair by her husband. It was left to Mr. Townsend, the owner of a signwriting business in Clacton, to rescue this family. Sadly he died after an accident only weeks later.

Mrs. Gage, who lived in The Village, clearly heard her dead mother say: 'Don't panic Mary'. Taking heed, she helped her sick husband and cat into the loft. Hours after scouring and probing the water for signs of rescue, they were hauled out through the roof.

Survey parties were sent out to track down any serviceable boats: some arrived on trucks and one came by wheelbarrow, pushed two miles by a young Clactonian on a trolley. Eight rowing boats belonging to Mr. E. Wellham of Jaywick Lane, who rented them out in the summer, were commandeered by the police.

By 5.45 p.m. on Sunday eight rescue boats were in action. Each boat was manned by a policeman, a volunteer, and a boatman. The first, launched from Jaywick Lane, at around 4.15 a.m. carried the Allum brothers, the fire brigade station officer, Mr. Gay, and a telephone engineer. Mr. Gay had been one of the first to arrive on the scene at around 3 a.m. and later collapsed from exhaustion, thereby ending up in hospital alongside those he had helped rescue.

The Red Cross set up a mobile canteen in Jaywick Lane. They gave out hot soup and endless cups of tea while those still trapped were told: 'Hold on, the firemen have arrived'.

Mr. Fawcett, a Clacton resident who had been woken by a boy scout, arrived in Jaywick bringing assistant scoutmaster C.H. Marsh with him. They commandeered a canvas canoe and, setting off in the direction of hysterical cries, saved a family of four. But only doors away, after smashing through a window, they found both occupants dead.

By this stage five or six survivors were being landed every minute. Many were half naked, covered only by curtains pulled off windows. A number had been recovered from half-submerged windows, while others had to be disentangled with difficulty from lengths of springy expanding wire.

As the hours dragged by exhausted Clacton and Wivenhoe men were relieved by men from Brightlingsea, Tiptree, Manningtree, Bradfield and Weeley.

St John's Ambulance driver Mr. Basil Fenn drove his only 'live case', 62-year-old former nurse Louise Kemp, from Grasslands to hospital. She had been woken by her cat 'Tinker', a 14-year-old veteran of the Second World War, who had pawed at Louise's face. They were trapped for 31 hours.

Hazel and Jack Wright, married just three months, grabbed a terrified kitten before they ran for safety after the water came over the wall in Point Clear Bay. 'I don't think we shall ever forget the moment we heard a shout around 6 a.m., and there in the darkness and phenomenal gale force wind were Dennis and Douglas Burns who we both knew, trying to bring a dinghy alongside. They had seen the proverbial flickering candle in the window; our prayers were answered.' Hazel had followed her mother's advice: 'If you're ever in trouble girl, put your hands together, say a prayer and trust in God'. Today almost seventy, Hazel wept when remembering that night.

Every bungalow was searched. Survivors were wrapped in blankets and taken by boat to a fleet of ambulances waiting in Jaywick Lane. From there they were driven to Clacton Hospital, where the boardroom was opened up. When all the beds were full nurses gave up their own beds to help out. Clactonians opened their purses, their doors and their hearts to the homeless: one young mum lifted up her sleeping baby and handed her pram over to another mother who had lost everything; a local clergyman stopped his car, took off his shoes and socks, and gave them to a barefoot man; another woman took her coat off and gave it to a shivering old lady without a word. Gifts of food, sweets, furniture, bedding and money poured in from as far off as Hong Kong. There were offers of sandbags and sandbaggers, drivers and transport.

Jane Gray, a transatlantic broadcaster, visited Jaywick. She gathered together some of the stories she had heard from survivors, and later sent a cablegram that read: 'Greetings from Canada, voices and stories touched our hearts. Sending food parcels, rush airmail list of names'.

The kindness and help shown to the distraught people was overwhelming. Canadian donations paid to carpet homes, and 17,000 extra copies of the local paper, the *East Essex Gazette*, sold all over the world. Its publisher, Messrs. A. Quick and Co., donated the value of these extra copies to the Flood Relief Fund.

Despite the many problems facing him, Mr. Hearn, Clerk to the Council, had Clacton hotels ready to accommodate 700 people by sunrise. Their stay was financed by Essex County Council. A warm bed, comfort and a hot cup of tea were waiting at: *The Glengariff*, 41; *The Grosvenor Court*, 59; *Oulton Hall*, 88; *The Hadleigh*, 80; *The Westcliff*, 70; *The Royal*, 27 and *The Osborn*, 30. Seventeen were found places in boarding houses, and 72 stayed in the Red Cross Hall.

Afterwards letters of thanks poured in to newspapers from survivors, many of whom were now staying at Valley Farm Camp. After the manager had telegraphed every owner to obtain consent, the whole site was put at the disposal of the relief authorities. The switch to turn the camp into summer occupation took just 24 hours. Eastern National buses pulled up on 4 February to take 115 survivors to the camp.

Superstitious folk who 'held their collar and did not swallow until they saw a dog' when seeing an ambulance could happily let go! Amid the ambulances called 'Ivy' and 'Hilda' a small black dog swam furiously after the rescue boat and then the ambulance that carried its master to hospital. This loyal friend was looked after by Mrs. Richardson at Sunny Corner Kennels, Little Clacton, until the RSPCA took over the welfare of all the animals.

'Nobby' Abbott, who lived in a sea-front chalet called 'Why Worry' after a winning greyhound, rescued worried-looking Rex, a shaggy brown and black dog belonging to his sister. The last animal rescued, it had survived without food for five days. Although wrapped in a warm blanket, it still looked worried even though it had the back seat of a police car all to itself. Rex only perked up after a pat on the head from Sir Stanley Holmes, M.P. for Harwich, who had arrived in Clacton at the same time as the dog.

The first question people asked once their families were safe was 'What about our pets?'. A survivor taken to Chelmsford Hospital from Clacton because she was so ill, fretted so much about her dog that an S.O.S. went out. Twelve-year-old Toby—a cross between a collie and a retriever—was eventually located floating on a broken-down bathroom door, alive, but only just!

83 Rescuer, 'Jimmy the Milk', tucks into ice cream with friends in the 1940s.

84 *Below left.* Survivors of the floods, newly-weds Hazel and Jack Wright.

85 *Below right.* Mr. Basil Fenn from the St John's Ambulance brigade. He took Louise Kemp, who had been trapped for 31 hours, to hospital.

The body loses heat to water 20 times faster than to air, and as a result people suffered from hypothermia and exposure. Likewise some people died due to complications that set in after the floods.

Clearly pets suffered as well. Although normally quick witted, some animals became suspicious and headed off in the opposite direction when rescuers tried to help them. A vet from Ilford PDSA, Mr. Jenkins, and his assistant Jim Whiting, saved many animals. They were helped by a local called Jim who used his 10ft. dinghy in the rescue.

Sometimes there was only a trail of muddy footsteps to guide them, but they still crawled on their hands and knees to lure animals from beneath chalets and overturned tables. They were usually petrified, after perhaps not hearing a human voice for days, and were hugged close for a moment before being put into pillowcases and later dropped at the Animal Rescue Centre.

A canary more dead than alive when rescued sang like an opera singer after food and warmth, cheering rescuers no end.

But well-meaning people, who mistook the bulging pillowcases for stolen goods sang their own sweet song—to the police. Jim hastily explained, before saving an artificial leg belonging to the local greengrocer, 'Sonny' Collingford. He wrapped this carefully in a sheet and handed it over to Sonny, who was found, sick as a parrot, hopping about on a broomstick.

Inspector Archer of the North-East Essex RSPCA, with help from an unemployed welder from Clacton who was his oarsman, bagged 22 cats, 14 dogs, four pigeons and a canary. Mr. H. Loveless, a Clacton vet, treated all rescued animals free of charge.

The BBC was criticised for ignoring the estate after the first broadcast at 1 p.m. on that Sunday. However some business people, concerned about possible damage to the holiday trade, believed that the less publicity Jaywick got the better.

BBC news commentators had toured up and down the distressed areas taking pictures and stories, but Jaywick was not included. On Monday evening their programmes included eyewitness stories from various areas. A BBC tour started in Yorkshire, then visited the Norfolk coast, King's Lynn, Southwold and other Suffolk areas, but then bypassed north-east Essex entirely to go straight to Foulness, Canvey, Sheerness and Whitstable.

Jaywick was also excluded when many eminent people came to the flooded areas to give sympathy. The Queen and the Duke of Edinburgh, the Queen Mother and Princess Margaret, the Duchess of Kent and the Home Secretary—all visited different sections of the stricken areas.

However, Miss M. Wilson, assistant secretary of the Canadian Red Cross, came to see Clacton and Jaywick for herself. The area had been selected by the National Red Cross as the one place in the United Kingdom to be visited and inspected officially. The Bishop of Colchester also visited.

Mr. and Mrs. Wolfe, having been notified of the disaster, were heading for Jaywick by 6 a.m. On arrival nobody had as yet been able to reach Brooklands. 'Adrian's Wall' had not broken, but the man who had it built was.

Jaywick lost 35 residents, Point Clear two. Shopkeepers Mr. and Mrs. Cresswell were discovered drowned by their 19-year-old son. A café owner, his mum had told him over the telephone: 'Save yourself, we're drowning'.

Five hundred people were rescued by boat. At 5.40 p.m. on Monday the rescue operation ceased, but the whirring of police motor boats continued and the grim search for the dead went on.

Wrapped in grey blankets, the dead were driven to a temporary mortuary in Clacton. Here Inspector N. Munson, Special Superintendent W.G. Boulton, and PC 'Timber' Wood worked on day and night duty. Frank Allum was brave enough to identify all the dead bodies. Although Jaywick was now sealed off, the police patrolled danger spots on a 24-hour watch. They allowed nobody into their homes that first weekend.

Later residents were allowed one visit to their homes to collect goods and valuables, having been issued with police permits. Inspections were made to check the individual electricity and gas supplies. Likewise the soundness of the buildings had to be checked. All these points had to be cleared before police allowed people to move back.

One old lady was rescued still clutching her Sunday joint. She insisted that she couldn't afford another one, but it was well known that she was one of the wealthiest ladies on the estate.

An 89-year-old chap whose wooden leg had floated out to sea taking his trousers along with it, cracked: 'I have been hard up and not had a shilling to put in my pocket—now I have no pocket to put my money in'. There were shivers on hearing about the policeman who picked up an open book lying on the floor of a victim's home: its title was *The Cruel Sea*.

Organisers worked full-time, and concerts and dances were put on to support the victims. Clacton Salvation Army Band played in the streets. A tea-party was arranged for children at St Paul's Hall, Clacton. One little girl, whose feet were blistered by being in the water for eight hours, was given a brand new doll.

Half the water had flowed back to the sea by Friday 6 February, but police still guarded the entrance to the estate and troops were ready to seal it off with barbed wire. Everybody waited for the floods to subside. When 'Operation Mop Up' got under way, members of Clacton's Round Table Association volunteered to help the old and infirm.

More than a million pounds worth of damage had been caused, and over 300 people were killed that night throughout the country; 100 died in Essex alone. The killer tide had made more than 300 breaches in the county's sea walls. More than 5,000 acres of farmland, were submerged. The Navy helped at Harwich, and the RAF helped out across the estuary at Felixstowe where a seaplane base had been devastated.

A survey in Jaywick had revealed that of the 600 buildings examined 200 were fine, with only slight damage; 150 were damaged but repairable; and 250 were very badly damaged. Restoration costs were paid in full. Moreover 85 per cent of the expenditure incurred improving existing defences was met by the Government. Victims got priority for building repairs.

The Essex Rivers Board, responsible for the defence of a 300-mile stretch of coastline, carried out emergency repairs between Colne Point and Leewick. Emergency measures which had been introduced in the aftermath of the 1949 floods were brought into force again.

One thousand million gallons of water had to be pumped from an area of approximately four square miles. 10,000 gallons were pumped out per minute. 30,000 people were involved in 'Operation Canute' as it was called. 120 airmen, 300 soldiers and 20 men from the council were employed to release the water. They used breaches and drained at low water, operating the sewage pumping station in Jaywick Lane for that purpose. Pumps were towed along Golf Green Road which was itself still flooded to a depth of two feet.

Work involved deepening breaches and then using bulkheads and sandbags to control these in accordance with the state of the tide. Prior to the floods the Board had a stock of 50,000 sand bags, but its stock rose to 10 million during the height of the clearing-up operation.

In March 1953, the Government produced legislation to provide for sea defence work in areas affected by the floods. Further work was carried out to raise the sea wall from Jaywick to Point Clear by two or three feet and a half a million pounds was earmarked for work in the Tendring Section (Grasslands) and beyond.

A memorial service was held at St James's Church, Clacton, where the address was given by the Bishop of Chelmsford. St Christopher's in Jaywick lost all its records but its bell was rescued by Mr. Ward, a local builder, who climbed onto the roof and brought it home tucked under his sweater for safety.

The Government took steps to plan a system of flood warnings in the future, and a new ruling was put into operation whereby the Chief Constable would be responsible for warning the public of further flooding.

Despite his bitter sadness at events, Mr. Wolfe was the guiding hand behind much of the work carried out during this painful time. Everything which had found its way into the dykes had to be hauled out. Thousands of cups of tea were brewed to keep people going, and cakes and cigarettes were handed out. A 'drop of the hard stuff' was considered essential after a chalet owner, whilst inspecting his property, tripped over and had to be fished out of the dyke. Although stinking and up to his neck in the contents of the Elsan toilets he had to laugh.

Despite everyone's efforts for many months the estate was in such a bad state that some avenues were called 'Suicide Alley'. There was stagnant water, sludge and inches of thick mud and slime everywhere; shovels were needed to clear it off carpets and curtains. The whole town stank. It was too much for some, and a number of shops and homes were put up for auction.

Although the Freeholders wrote to the council several times asking it to drain the estate and allow them part of the local relief money, its response was slow. The association, resenting what they saw as the council's high-handed attitude, decided in July that if no action had been taken by that November, they would give the council an ultimatum: 'Help us or we go to the Ministry!'. They remembered that within hours of the catastrophe the Prime Minister had announced that the costs of rehabilitation would be borne by the nation. Subscriptions to the National Tempest and Flood Relief Fund built up. The Lord Mayor's Flood Relief Fund paid out in the region of £2 million, the taxpayer almost £400,000. Insurance companies also paid out, although it was estimated that only a fifth of all the people on the estate were covered.

The estate finally received £197,340. This great sum went a long way towards putting the estate right. By Whitsun, the estate was open for business.

In the Birthday Honours List later that year Harmer received the Queen's Commendation, while Special Constable Batchelor and Mrs. Allard each received OBEs. For others the knowledge that they had 'done their bit' was ample reward. However, even today there are many who remember that night vividly, and are bitter and disappointed at the lack of official recognition for so many.

Coronation Day

In spite of cutbacks because of the floods, on 23 May 1953 800 Clacton lights were switched on along the sea-front in time for Coronation Day. Buntings and flags alone set the council back £1,500.

The death of King George VI on 6 February 1952 had brought Princess Elizabeth back from Kenya, where she had been on the first leg of a Commonwealth tour. Thanks to television and the cinema, she was the first British Sovereign truly to be crowned, as the rubric requires, 'in the sight of all the people'.

FLOOD WARNINGS
Official Statement

THE Government is to take steps to plan a system of flood warnings in the future.

This statement was given in the House of Commons on Wednesday by the Home Secretary, Sir David Maxwell Fyfe.

Sir David said: " There has been criticisms in certain quarters that no adequate warning was given to the public in the areas concerned. This country has been fortunate in not having suffered any ordeal of this kind during this century and no Government in that time had thought it necessary to organise a public warning system for this purpose.

" I have, however, given instructions that the question of devising a warning system should be explored as a matter of urgency, and I hope to be able to make a statement soon. There are obvious difficulties in deciding what areas should be warned and the time at which the warning should be given."

86   A press cutting about the 1953 flooding.

87 Workmen carrying out repairs on the sea-front after a wave smashed a 30-yard hole through the concrete sea wall during the 1953 floods.

Many Jaywick people, celebrating for the first time in months, boarded the special coronation train from Clacton to take their place on the Coronation route.

The Man Who Cried

1962 was the coldest year recorded since 1919 and was only 17 days old when the hard businessman with the fierce blue eyes and grand ideas died. Frank Stedman would have been 88 the following March. Elizabeth died seven years later, aged 94.

Ken Gibbons, who attended Stedman's funeral, knew the whole family as a child and had worked for Stedman for many years. He said of him:

He was a good and clever man who would help anybody out—all that family would, especially 'Minny'. He was always dipping into his pocket for charity but never broadcast the fact. Who do you think financed the many court actions taken over the years? It wasn't always the associations or residents.

The Stedman grave is tucked away in a bright sunlit corner of Burrs Road cemetery, Clacton.

'The Jaywick Decision' had created 2,200 properties. Although Stedman, who had lived in 27 homes, never quite realised his dream for all of the estate, thousands have him to thank for carefree holidays and their own place in the sun. There was nothing in Stedman's notes about loving 'the children of Jaywick', but love them he did. It had been cold on Sunday 1 February 1953, and he had cried.

8

Mixed Blessings

The Inn Thing

The estate was built by people of limited means with their own hands, but it had found its feet and was established as a happy holiday resort. Motorists were able to use main roads such as the A12, A120 and A133 to get to within a few miles of Jaywick. Clacton had direct lines to Cambridge and the Midlands, with a regular Saturday service to Birmingham and Leicester.

Dennis & Sons sold out to Truman's who used their premises as a bottling plant during the war. They later turned it into a public house, naming it after the 1954 Derby winner, a 33-1 outsider ridden by 18-year-old Lester Pigott— 'The Never Say Die'.

In all the pubs and clubs weekenders sang 'Magic Moments', 'Singing In The Rain' and 'Wheel of Fortune'. Then the band, towards the end of the evening, would often strike up 'Run Rabbit Run' or 'Horsey, Horsey', old wartime songs which always raised a big cheer. Onlookers clapped along with the music: 'Horsey, horsey, don't you stop, just let your feet go clippety clop'. Finally, flushed and sweating, the dancers flopped down in a heap onto their chairs.

By 1956 the estate had a second public house. Mr. G. Flaunty, a tall impressive-looking businessman and local councillor, had opened the *Mermaid Inn*, a two-storey building painted sky-blue. The interior had fishing nets strung across the room which were filled with artificial starfish, seaweed, crabs, and blood-red lobsters. A captain's wheel hung on the wall of the building that faced Brooklands Club.

Flaunty, who had bought and sold Golf Green Garage, rebuilt the pub himself. It had once been a grocery and an off-licence. He had to run it without water for seven years, so was forced to carry water on a water-lorry from his nearby home each day. The Freeholders, objecting to the competition, refused him access to their water mains.

Flaunty considered that there was a need for a second public house in Jaywick because only members could use the Club or the Farmhouse. Objections were made, but he stayed in business.

Holiday-makers loved the farmhouse wines he stocked, and after a few glasses of 'Mead', 'Elderberry' or 'Highland Fling' they kicked like a mule. His merry punters didn't care if the water came from hell as long as it arrived. One red-headed holidaymaker who has returned to Jaywick year in year out, always taking home a thick dark green bottle of 'Mead', blames the birth of her daughter, Dawn Julie, my own beautiful niece, on Flaunty's wicked wines. 'It had nothing to do with me' Flaunty insisted, with a twinkle in his eye.

21 Years On

The children of the war years had come of age. So too had the Freeholders who went to town celebrating their 21st birthday in 1951.

Brooklands Club was packed with young moody 'Teddy Boys'. They wore long drape jackets with velvet collars and cuffs, drainpipe trousers, and thick suede shoes. Rock and Roll had arrived. 'Only You', 'The Great Pretender', and other hits of the times blared from the stage. People rocked away until, with one wave from the MC, the band brought things to a standstill: Mr. Wolfe had something to say.

Whenever he was asked if Jaywick was a liability to Clacton, he would answer: 'No, for it provides £20,000 in rates in return for little service, practically only a dust collection, and there is always a surplus to balance the Clacton budget. Jaywick further supplies £100,000 of trade to the town every season.' Mr. Wolfe spoke that evening of the 'Tooth and Nail' drive in operation, which aimed at bringing better roads, street lighting, adequate sea defences and just rate expenditure to Jaywick. He was angered by the award of £250,000 to Holland-on-Sea for sea defences, when Jaywick had received nothing.

On 5 December 1957 the council had discussed the resolution of the Freeholders relating to responsibility for the maintenance of the coastal protection works in front of the Brooklands section. It decided that no decision could be reached until the various legal and practical implications had been discussed with the appropriate officials of the Government departments concerned. The Freeholders were unhappy with the delay and passed a resolution at their next AGM which read:

> this 24th AGM records that another year has passed without the authorities who are legally empowered to protect the coast line carrying out their statutory obligations, and again protests against the delay in completing these negotiations. It urges the desire of its members that the Brooklands section shall be recognised as an inland drainage district, and it expresses the willingness of its members to pay the special dues which would be levied by the Board by way of drainage rates over a period of years on all properties within the protected areas.

It records its appreciation of the Ministry of Agriculture, Fisheries and Food for its assistance and directives during the negotiations with the Essex Rivers Board over the repair works necessary to the Brooklands sea wall at this juncture. It also records its appreciation of the Board's co-operation in dealing with the present works.

The Board agreed to undertake the work. Its decision was subject to a Ministry grant contributing to the expenditure, and the Freeholders meeting the balance of the costs.

The Board wrote to the council to explain that they had taken the view that, if the Brooklands wall was to be maintained or improved as a permanent work, it would be unwise to delay major work on it. They considered the work to be beyond the capacity of the Freeholders Association and felt it unlikely that the council would promote a scheme in relation to this particular sea wall under the Coast Protection Act of 1949 because such a scheme would present many problems and would be difficult to administer. They came to the conclusion that the most direct course would be for them to assume responsibility for the wall and create an inland drainage area for the Brooklands section of Jaywick under section 4 (1) (b) of the Land Drainage Act.

That same month the council met the Ministry of Housing and Local Government and the future of the estate was discussed. Officials of the Local Planning Authority (Essex County Council) and the Board were present. The outcome was that little, if any, financial assistance was likely to come from government sources or the County Council towards compensation that would have to be paid by Clacton in respect of the acquisition of land and the execution of works on the estate.

9

New Faces

At Easter 1964 hundreds of 'Mods and Rockers' clashed in Clacton town centre, causing thousands of pounds worth of damage. In that year also Harold Wilson, the man with hang-dog looks and clipped Yorkshire accent, at 48 became the youngest P.M. this century.

When a third public house opened on the estate there was a party. Everybody was given a present at *The Sheldrake*, which had been built by a local businessman, Mr. E. Sheldrake. He had run a taxi-service and café on Meadow Way. This new pub was located near the site of the old bus terminus, and close to 'Sweet Tina's', a curtain shop owned by Londoner Terry.

In opening his taxi-service and café in the 1950s, Sheldrake had upset Stedman because the restrictions and stipulations that no business should be carried out without his consent had not been respected. Stedman asked for a mandatory injunction compelling Sheldrake to remove his business from Meadow Way. Mr. Harman, in the Chancery Division, refused his injunction. Giving judgement he said:

there was no doubt that restrictions on building land had in the past performed a very useful function. It might however be doubted whether in these days they were not rather outmoded and whether it would not be better for the whole question of use and enjoyment to be left to the local authority and the town planning regulations.

88   *The Sheldrake* public house was built in the 1960s.

89 *The Three Jays* was built on the edge of the estate in the 1960s. Originally a Nissen hut stood on the site which was used by the army during the Second World War.

The Three Jays, a Nissen hut used during the war to accommodate troops, became the estate's fourth and last public house. It was built in the 1960s, when the Tudor Estate was being developed and the idea of a Tudor Village was abandoned—the green had been built over during the late 1950s. *The Three Jays* was opened and managed by Trumans. It is situated at Crossways.

Essex Police Authority was responsible for maintaining law and order, and was becoming more and more concerned about the increasing crime rate on the estate. For example, the post office was broken into and £3,431 was stolen.

The Tower Caravan Park
The estate is located between the important areas of Clacton and Point Clear/St Osyth, which has the biggest concentration of holiday caravans in the district. 1963 saw the opening of the Tower Caravan Park, which lies on the western edge of New Town.

Although not part of Stedman's Jaywick the new park, which has in its centre the Martello Tower from which it took its name, is considered an asset. Many residents use its launderette because the estate no longer has

one. Likewise children often nip across to swim or use the play area provided, because the estate has neither. The park also has a club and other amusements as well as prize bingo.

Mr. B. Matthews, a former school teacher and today a respected Clacton magistrate, purchased the 45-acre site including a 2½-acre site used previously as a camping site and later a caravan park by a small company which rented out 60 vans. Mr. Matthews today rents 525 static vans, and has a licence for 100 touring vans.

Council's Five-Year Development Plan
In May 1961 the council approved in principle a five-year plan for works in Jaywick costing in the region of £370,000, of which approximately £270,000 would be recoverable from the frontages. The plan was due to be completed in the year ending 31 March 1966.

Main drains were installed in The Village. This meant that New Town was now the only section on the estate remaining unsewered.

Because of legal and practical difficulties the council was prevented from carrying out all the work it intended doing. Its intention to carry out the second phase was dependent on proposals to widen streets, but this didn't happen. A change of local authority put a stop to all work.

Three hundred residents who had handed over between £30 and £260 for the street improvements had been promised in writing that the work would be done. They were disgusted when the new authority refused to acknowledge the former authority's decision and refund their money. A spokesman for the new authority said: 'the impression that we would take over these roads is categorically denied and no such commitment exists either morally or in law'. Those concerned were legally advised they had no choice other than to accept the situation.

In 1969 grateful members presented Mr. Wolfe with a salver engraved 'in appreciation of services so freely given'. In that year he had a one-man exhibition of his water-colours in London. In the same year his bronze plaque of William Morris, who influenced him greatly, was fixed to William Morris Towers at Essex University, so named at his suggestion.

Although he had now been elected to the council, he continued to fight for further improvements to Brooklands sea defences. He bombarded Parliament with memoranda which led to its recognition of this new line of defence. He played a large part in the eventual take-over of the walls by the Board, and was co-opted to the River Board's works committee in 1965.

The Ratepayers lost their secretary, Mrs. D. Ready, who left the association to care for 10 boys she had fostered. In time their hard work began to pay off. The clearest demonstration of this was the building of the Public Hall. Located on Golf Green Road, it serves as a library, a doctor's surgery and a social hall. Completed in 1966, it cost the council £12,000; the Ratepayers contributed towards the extension added in 1970.

All Saints' Catholic Church was built at Crossways in the 1960s, but wedding bells didn't ring out in Jaywick until the Methodist Church opened in 1967. This was the only church to have a licence to conduct the service. Jaywick's first bride, Pat Deer of Flowers Way, a care assistant in a Clacton nursing home, married Mr. J. Hennick of Bocking Elms.

Jaywick Methodist Church was built by Messrs. Sadler & Sons of Ipswich on the site of a 300-year-old cottage. It was dedicated on 11 March 1967. The organ was an anonymous gift.

Rubbish Jaywick

The council's redevelopment plans for New Town dragged on. At a June 1955 meeting a revised scheme was outlined for its development as a very large holiday centre to overcome the present difficulties. A scheme had already been discussed but around £300,000 would be needed to provide a satisfactory layout and a proper sewerage scheme.

This latest scheme entailed redevelopment of cleared areas as a funfair and amusement park along with a camping site and the necessary shopping facilities. As an alternative the Brooklands area could be converted into a boating lake. Nothing happened.

In February 1967 what was fast looming on the horizon was the possibility that an 80-acre rubbish tip was to be sited at Jaywick. The council had already turned down the gravel pits at Great Holland and land at St Osyth as being unsuitable. It was to be sited to the west of the area at the back of the estate, on land belonging to Hutleys Ltd.

Women wore Mary Quant miniskirts, bouffant hair-does and sexy shiny boots in a variety of colours, but nobody would wear this. The thought of a rubbish tip enraged the residents who started collecting money to set up their own committee to fight the proposal. Their objections included the smell, the fact that it would be a breeding ground for flies, and the loss of value to property in the area.

A protest march was held on 22 March 1967 through Clacton. Supporters waved placards and carried dustbin lids on their way to a public inquiry in the Assembly Hall on Marine Parade. This only accommodated 40 people, and the committee complained that the Princes Theatre would have been a more suitable venue—their opponents on the council were well aware that circulars had been sent to 2,800 objectors. Old Contemptible, Mr. W.R. Walters, a member of the committee, carried a Union Jack into the hall for the three-day inquiry, which was conducted by inspectors from the Ministry of Housing and Local Government. Several councillors, including Councillor C.H. Ball, attended.

The council, which was represented by Mr. A. Cripps Q.C., had been advised by Councillor Wolfe to back down because the committee had the support of a report from the Land Commission. If they continued they would have to fight some 2,500 residents; his advice fell on deaf ears.

Domestic and trade refuse collected by the council was disposed of by controlled tipping. An incinerator plant had been installed at Rush Green in 1930, when the average refuse collection amounted to 4,200 tons per annum; by 1967 it was 14,000 tons. Councillor Ball argued that the present tipping site at St Martin's Farm, St Osyth, could no longer be used. He stressed that the council had taken much advice over possible solutions, and claimed that the matter was now urgent.

Mr. J.L. Lowe, representing the committee, was unimpressed by Ball's arguments. He reminded the inquiry that in 1934 Stedman had agreed to reserve 30 acres at the rear of Brooklands as a permanent open space to over-come the density problem without reducing the number of bungalows.

Mr. Desmond-Wright, acting for Stedman's trustees who owned part of the land, declared that the council were trying to back out of this agreement. Mr. A.R. Baker, a local builder living at Crossways, whose house was only 200 yards from the proposed tip, was concerned and worried that people would not buy property anywhere near a rubbish tip. Mr. B. Hutley, a partner in the firm E. & A. Hutley, said that 120 animals used that area and argued that a tip would reduce the grazing land by a quarter of an acre. The committee won the day.

By 1969 Neil Stedman, Frank's grandson, was a councillor for Jaywick and a partner in his grandfather's estate office. During these negotiations he was not a member of the committee, but left the room when the council considered purchasing the foreshore rights. Once owned by the trustees of the manor of St Osyth, they were offered to the council for £7,500, which wanted them for £5,000. The offer was refused and they were later purchased for £10,000 by Carradine Protin Ltd. of London.

Residents & Ratepayers Association

Brooklands Club was slipping in popularity and the Freeholders had to ask members for their support to keep it going.

The population was increasing, and a third association was formed during the early 1970s. Called the Residents & Ratepayers Association, it took over all work connected with Elsan closets and set up a night security patrol of two women with dogs. They improved and main-tained street lighting, and hoped to take over the refuse collection. Council lorries, in their view, damaged the roads. Chairman Moorcroft wanted improved conditions in Jaywick simply because she loved it. I shall refer to the Residents & Ratepayers Association as the Residents Association throughout this book.

10

'Mi Casa Es Su Casa'—My House is Your House

A Public Disgrace

Places such as Peacehaven, Canvey Island and Jaywick were hated by local authorities who named them 'plotlands'. They were seen as sprawling shanty towns, seaside slums, and a national and local disgrace. The 1947 Town and Country Planning Act controlled new development and halted future plotlands, but those already in existence remained a head-ache.

Although over the years there were hints and threats, nobody on the estate really expected any action to be taken. However, at a routine council meeting on 6 January 1971, New Town was declared a clearance area under the terms of the Public Health Act. Compulsory clearance orders were issued on the grounds that the whole of the area was unsanitary and dilapidated. 'My House is Your House' is an old East End saying, but now heartsick owners were being forced out.

Plot-owners were paid £150 each for their properties, but this represented the site value only. These payments were later increased to £200, but even this sum did not amount to the full market value which the council had promised to pay.

Mr. R. Carroll, Chairman of the Freeholders, described the decision as 'morally indefensible'. He was one of nature's gents. In the article 'A Chalet by The Sea', *Observer Magazine*, 15 June 1975, Tim Street-Porter recorded that Mr. Carroll had been tipped off by a journalist friend from the local newspaper about the meeting.

PRICES OF SITES

Varying from 20 ft., 26 ft. and 40 ft. frontage and 60 ft. depth.

THE SITES

have mostly 26 ft. frontage and 60 ft. depth, many have more, some have less, but the great majority are the size stated.

PRICES

MEADOW WAY	..	..	..	from £48
JASMINE WAY	..	..	..	„ £68
GARDEN ROAD	..	..	..	„ £78
CORNFLOWER ROAD	..	..	..	„ £68
ROSEMARY WAY	..	..	..	„ £68
GLEBE WAY	..	..	..	„ £68
FLOWERS WAY	..	..	..	„ £78
LAVENDER WALK	..	..	..	„ £78
WILLOW WAY	..	..	..	„ £78
CHURCH ROAD	..	..	..	„ £85
BEACH ROAD	..	..	..	„ £120
THE CLOSE	..	..	..	„ £150

A few sites are still for sale with beach frontage.

Main Drainage and Gas, Water and Electric Light are all available.

VIEWING can be effected at any time without notice. The local Estate Office at Jaywick is open every day, including week-ends and holidays. Applicants can be met at the station with a car upon notice being given, and special attendance given to any such appointments made.

FULLER PARTICULARS AND PLAN on application to the Resident Agent, Mr. D. L. Stedman, Jaywick, Clacton-on-Sea. Phone: Clacton 497.

Office in London for convenience of those who would like to make enquiries before coming down :—

STEDMAN & CLARKE,
108, GUILDFORD STREET (Gray's Inn Rd. end), W.C.1.
Phone: Terminus 4704.

90   Property specification, The Village 1935.

Hoping councillors would justify his belief in their integrity by refraining from taking this step, he argued that:

> If they did not take this step, the association would be prepared—as they always have been— to discuss measures for resolving the problems of Brooklands and Grasslands (New Town).
>
> We want to express our abhorrence at the methods the council consider using in invoking the purchase. For, and let there be no misunderstanding about this, if the council carry out their intention it will mean that every Freeholder—and that includes many old-age pensioners who bought a bungalow with their life savings—would receive only a fraction of the money they have invested.
>
> Remember, this desire for redevelopment does not ultimately mean more houses for those in need. The plan is still only for holiday bungalows, and as speculative development, Clacton Council could hardly develop the area themselves. This intention is to take from the Freeholders, thereby inflicting on them considerable financial losses, presumably selling to a private developer, also making a profit.

With some 770 home-owners to be protected and 96 chalets demolished, he advised legal action and so the fight for Jaywick began.

On Sunday 24 September 1972, two days before a public inquiry was held on the matter, Mr. Carroll reported at the Freeholders' AGM that:

> Council do not want our land so they can build houses for the needy. They are under the impression that under the provision of the 1957 Housing Act they can acquire our land at £4,000 an acre, and then sell it on the open market at between £50,000 and £60,000 an acre. It has been stated by a number of people in local government that the area of Brooklands and Grasslands (New Town) is the most valuable site on the coast of Essex.
>
> Collectively we own it: collectively we paid £100,000 to protect it by building a sea wall: and collectively we contribute £5,000 every year for the maintenance of that wall. But for our collective efforts this most valuable site would be under water. For 40 years we have done so much and the council so little. And now they seek to destroy us. It is difficult to believe that councillors elected throughout those past 40 years to represent and protect, could so fail in their responsibilities to a small section of the community.

At the same meeting, Mr. A.A. Wolfe reported that:

> The policy now being adopted by council to acquire the properties and land on the Brooklands and Grasslands areas by compulsory purchase is being resisted collectively by your association. Council contributed nothing in money or brains to build the 1950 sea defence wall that provided a good access road to Grasslands. Council contributed nothing to subsequent efforts to get the straight front line recognised as the line of sea defence, which was accomplished when the Board set up the Brooklands Internal Drainage Board. They asked me to be its Chairman and arrange for the present wall to be built to its present high standard and the area to be recognised as liable to sea defence rating and therefore 'as part of England'.
>
> As soon as this was completed and there was no question of the area's impermanence, the association sent resolutions sponsored by me from each of its AGMs asking for the amenities which council is by law compelled to provide, namely main sewers, main water, surface drainage, etc.
>
> For nearly 10 years they ignored or delayed any practical answers to these requests. They now think to make a compulsory purchase order, mainly on the grounds that our bungalows are without the basic amenities they themselves should have provided. If they succeed they will gain a most valuable site close to the sea for next to nothing which they admit they intend selling to a developer—not, as is usual when such orders are made, to provide council houses for the needy! No, because this is not a housing area, it is a holiday area, and these are not houses in the ordinary sense and should not come under the Housing Act. The whole matter with an enlightened council could have been covered under Planning Acts which could have dealt with any dilapidations, and left those who look after their properties, and enjoy their bungalow by the sea, to continue to do so and have the basic modern facilities as well.

On 26 September 1972 objectors (including myself and my husband, both members of the Freeholders Association) packed into the Princes Theatre, Clacton. There were over 500 plot-owners on the first day alone. By now Mr. Wolfe was very ill, but Junior Counsel Mr. Costello and the London barrister, Mr. G.S. Dobry Q.C., waited to defend Jaywick.

The inquiry was conducted by Mr. A.S. Barnes, Inspector of the Department of the Environment, who was also asked to consider the Freeholders' complaint that under the Public Health Act of 1936 the council was at fault by failing to provide water supply and main drainage to the area.

The council was represented by Planning Officer Spence and other council officials. The inquiry brought to the surface the various arguments for and against the acquisition, and the following two schemes for the redevelopment of New Town were constantly referred to:

Plan No. 4044/7: A plan submitted by the Essex County Planning Department in the early 1960s that envisaged demolishing all the properties on Brooklands and Grasslands (New Town), incorporating 14 acres to the north of Brooklands, closing the front access road, using the present dirt road that runs at the back of the old sea wall from Lion Point to Grasslands as the main service road and building approximately 657 chalets.

Plan No. 3306: A council scheme that retained the present layout of Brooklands and Grasslands providing a main drainage system. There was a subsequent amendment to this scheme considered, following a survey by council officials, where selected bungalows would be compulsorily purchased and demolished to reduce the density of the properties in the area. This amendment was not produced at the inquiry.

Mr. Dobry complained throughout the hearing because he had not been supplied with documents used as evidence by the council. He also complained that the council had not put up top witnesses.

Mr. Spence asked the Inspector not to lose sight of the fact that the orders were for slum clearance. The facts spoke for themselves: it was no answer to say the dwellings could be rendered fit. He asked that the order be confirmed, and acknowledged that documents had not been produced in the normal way. Regarding a letter from the association to the Town Clerk which had not been read out, he declared that the letter had not stated that it should be read out. He concluded by saying, 'Authorities using Part 3 were never required to set out their proposals. It is no answer to our case to say that redevelopment is expensive; it is not expensive to us. Market value is too expensive to us, but site value is not.'

Mrs. Wolfe argued:

The association had built a sea wall and laid down roads for the two areas. The occupation of the areas had only been possible by the voluntary work of many people on the association. This area has a record of a community always fighting to protect itself, and we contend that it is an injustice for it to be dealt with in the way proposed. The land would not be there to acquire if it had not been for the 1950 sea wall which was accomplished by the efforts of my husband, who has given nearly a quarter of a century of service to this community.

The only facilities lacking were those the council had failed to provide, yet the council receives annually from the area £20,000 in rates. Is it reasonable that 691 bungalows that are in good or fair condition should be demolished because they offend the planner's eye?

The 89 that are unfit could be dealt with under discontinuance orders, and the vast majority would not be sacrificed for the minority. This community has for too long suffered the slings and arrows of outrageous fortune and it is time it had a break, and was provided with the standard amenities by the council.

With all the voluntary work that has gone into the preservation of this area by the people in this community, it is indefensible and unreasonable for the council to pluck it like a ripe plum just when its main difficulties have been solved.

Under Dobry's cross-examination it was revealed that the Planning Officer for the Essex County Council had not been consulted about making the clearance area. Likewise the council's Junior Public Health Officer knew nothing about District Council plans for sewering New Town, or why after 40 years the council had suddenly decided to use section 42 of the Housing Act.

He reported, after a detailed inspection of the area, that 297 bungalows were in good order, 192 required minor repairs and 202 needed repair or improvements. Eighty-five were poor.

91   Freeholders badge from the 1930s.

The Ministry of Health, after a cursory look over the area, was of the opinion that 500 bungalows were in a dilapidated state and should all be pulled down. They agreed that main drains and running water should have been supplied but had not recommended it.

A Deputy Engineer and Surveyor acting for the council did provide an estimate for the introduction of sewerage for Brooklands in the context of the development scheme. He had no idea how much it would cost to supply water, but the sewerage alone would cost £100,000. He admitted that to sewer New Town would be the least expensive scheme and also satisfactory to the Freeholders. However, Mr. Spence argued that the Freeholders could not afford to put main drainage in themselves, only to learn that a loan of £200,000 had been offered to the association before the clearance order for that very purpose.

No minutes of the council meeting held on 17 February 1971 were produced at the hearing when the decision to clear the area was supposed to have been ratified. In summing up Dobry declared that the cost of providing main services would be little more than the cost of clearing the site and rehousing the occupants. With regard to the classification of the area as 'unfit', he claimed that there were regulations under the Public Health Act which applied specifically to summer houses being used permanently, but that the council had ignored these. He questioned how the area could be developed when the roads and a large area in the middle remained in private hands. He also pointed out that a pumping station had been built at Lion Point in 1964. In conclusion he claimed that the council was not interested in public health, nor the welfare of the people in the area; it was interested only in money. It had taken this action for monetary, not humanitarian, reasons.

He asked for the council to be found at fault in respect of the Public Health Act. In addition he asked that an order be made for main drainage and water, and for confirmation that the formal requirements of Part 3 had not been complied with and as such were invalid and ultra vires.

Local business was represented at the inquiry. Mr. P. Hammlin Q.C., appearing for Mr. G. Flaunty of the *Mermaid Inn*, claimed that the only consistent feature of the last 30 years had been the continued protest from the Freeholders that the council should provide the services.

Mr. J. Barnes, appearing for four objectors, said:

> The council only regarded these properties as houses instead of holiday chalets when the question of a clearance area came up. Council did not approach their duties under the Housing Act in a judicial spirit, the order they made is ultra vires and bad in law.

Mr. Smith, appearing for several objectors, said:

> It is difficult to understand how circumstances that have existed for nearly 40 years have overnight become so bad that drastic action such as clearance must take place as a matter of urgency.

The inquiry was over. On 2 May 1974 the residents of New Town learned they could stay. Mr. Barnes had spent days in Jaywick and had reported: 'Here were worthy citizens, with a high degree of community organisation, who, just because their houses were substandard, should not be pushed around'. The council was criticised for its dawdling over the water supply and the huge discrepancy regarding the state of the bungalows. That clearance was not the way to tackle the problem was a view held by many.

The inquiry had cost the Freeholders £7,500. They met to celebrate at Mile End, London, instead of their usual venue of Brooklands. Mr. Carroll was presented with an illuminated address and an engraved tankard in appreciation of his work. When he rose to address them everybody stood up and joined in the thunderous applause. He spoke for them all when he claimed, 'We took on the big boys, and we won!'.

11

The Cinderella of the Essex Coast

Local Government Changes

As a result of local government reorganisation, from 1974 Anglian Water Authority (AWA) had direct responsibility for water supply and sewage disposal in the area.

From 1 April 1974, Clacton Urban District Council was dissolved and its authority was vested in the new Tendring District Council, based at Harwich. (I shall refer to the new Tendring District Council as New Tendring throughout this book.)

New Tendring, like all other local authorities, consists of two main elements—the elected councillors and the unelected officers. All major decisions have to be taken by councillors, but day-to-day decisions are often taken by officers in accordance with agreed council policies or under regulations made by the Government.

At this stage, the official name of the estate was changed back to the one word, Jaywick. Whatever its name, its reputation was suffering from greedy landlords who let properties out in such a bad state that holiday-makers complained time and time again to the Citizens' Advice Bureau. Many had not been told of the lack of piped water and the Elsan toilets. Although the Freeholders investigated every complaint and the situation did improve, the estate had by now acquired an unwanted reputation.

92   The old sluice, which featured in a 1936 High Court case.

To the distress of the many residents who improved their property and took pride in their environment, lowered standards and other problems led to the estate being stigmatised. It was referred to as the last shanty town in the country.

The years had certainly taken their toll. Parts of the estate looked faded, and many bungalows were badly in need of repair and a pot of paint. Outsiders, many of whom had never visited Jaywick, began to knock it. Television rental companies refused to rent sets to people from the estate, but more importantly its residents found it difficult to get work when they revealed their addresses.

Elderly folk, under the umbrella of the Ratepayers and Community Associations and Jaywick Community Association, were more fortunate. There were numerous activities organised for them in Golf Green Hall. Mr. Fred Damon, who was Chairman of the Ratepayers for six years, was made their President. He later became Chairman of the Jaywick Community Association which acts as a steering committee for the five clubs in the area.

Bus and taxi-drivers, referring to New Town as Dodge City, complained about entering it. It was also called Crime City, although Clacton Police said recently that the increasing crime rate in Jaywick—there were 92 domestic burglaries in 1994—is no worse than anywhere else in Essex.

Jaywick children were easy targets for school bullies, who teased that they lived in huts without main drains, in an area with unmade roads and without proper street lighting. During heavy storms there were often taunts of: 'Don't hurry home, your hut will have been blown over by now'.

National and local newspapers took to taking swipes at the estate and its residents. Likewise television crews would come along and upset them time and time again.

Mr. P. Harding has had a home in Jaywick since 1938. One of two councillors for Jaywick in 1974, he called Jaywick 'The Cinderella of the Essex Coast'. He arranged a trip for other local councillors to visit the area, but when only 22 out of 60 showed up, he commented:

'They don't want to know about Jaywick—and don't know what to do with it'. He claimed they were still sulking over the inquiry.

It has recently been acknowledged that Jaywick suffers from the sort of problems more usually seen in inner-city areas. In 1977 a representative of the housing charity Shelter acknowledged the problem of shanty town slums, and revealed that those in Jaywick were among the worst they had ever seen.

Housing Policy—Minute 60

In accordance with the Housing Act of 1957 all local authorities were required to give reasonable preference to persons who occupied insanitary or overcrowded houses, who had large families, or who lived under unsatisfactory housing conditions. New obligations were also introduced by sections 4 and 5 of the Housing (Homeless Persons) Act of 1977.

In June 1978 the New Tendring housing sub-committee recommended that: 'no further applications be considered from persons residing in properties between Brooklands and Grasslands, the south side of Crossways and West of Golf Green Road, Jaywick'. Neither press nor public attended the meeting when this decision was taken, nor was there any record of it in the New Tendring minutes. As a result nobody told the people of Jaywick.

Jaywick's local councillor, Mr. J. Hill, had recommended the resolution in order to stop people from outside the area deliberately moving into substandard accommodation locally, with the sole intention of gaining council housing.

When the decision was made public people complained that they were being deprived of their civil rights. The Chairman of the Ratepayers, Mr. Damon, asked that the decision be rescinded but was refused. He argued that: 'we have been left out in the cold in our part of the world; it is about time Jaywick was put back on the map. We want recognition of the area.' He complained to the local ombudsman that 'New Tendring had acted with prejudice in refusing to consider applications for council housing from persons residing in a certain defined area which the association represents'.

The senior officer in the New Tendring's housing department had said that applications from Jaywick were mostly from families who were unaware of a demand from any elderly people for accommodation.

An officer of the commission carried out an investigation early in 1980 and found that, over the previous three years, only 37 applications for rehousing had been received from the area. Fifty-one files on applications for housing from residents in Jaywick were examined. Twenty-seven were from old-age pensioners and four were from couples with no children despite the housing officer's comments. The Ratepayers won the day and New Tendring was found guilty of maladministration.

Sea Defence—1978/86/88

Since 1974 the AWA had installed a system designed to give the area maximum warning when floods were imminent: when tides rose above a certain level eight sirens would sound and patrol cars with public address systems would go round warning the area. Normally the police were also notified by the Meteorological Office of a risk of flooding. However a storm of protest blew up over the warning systems, after floods had occurred at New Year 1978 with no prior warning. Seventy-foot waves battered Clacton pier and caused damage estimated at nearly £3-4 million. Beach huts which brought in some £40,000 in annual revenue were destroyed.

Golf Green Road was under water after the high tide reached 17ft., just 2ft. less than in the 1953 floods. It had carried away the beach and left the wall exposed, yet no siren warning was issued.

Chief Superintendent Ray Long of Clacton Police did consider evacuation, but decided it was not necessary. People were called on, told where the water was and assistance was given. Afterwards the Ratepayers decided to set up their own system to evacuate the area in the event of flooding, to work in conjunction with that of the police and New Tendring Council. This system, the brainchild of Ratepayers' Chairman, Mr. Fred Damon, was put into operation at the earliest opportunity.

The plan involved the use of street wardens who were given a list of roads which were

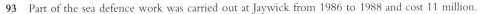

93   Part of the sea defence work was carried out at Jaywick from 1986 to 1988 and cost 11 million.

their individual responsibility in the event of a flood. They were to account for all residents in their area, paying particular attention to disabled people, who would need extra help to get out of their houses if the situation arose. The chief warden was Mr. R. Druce of the Ratepayers, whose wife helps co-ordinate the year's programme for the five clubs in the area. The plan is no longer in operation due mainly to lack of volunteers. It began with 12 wardens but, according to Mr. Druce, to cover Jaywick adequately there should be at least one hundred.

When fieldwork was carried out to discover the condition of Jaywick's sea defences, a substantial amount of material was discovered to have been deposited against many of the walls. Groynes were spaced about 180ft. apart, but many were in a bad state of disrepair and could not be fully effective in deflecting waves from the walls. Some were made entirely of wood, while others were constructed of concrete and wood.

Sea walls showed much variety in their design and construction. Afterwards the sea walls fronting West Clacton, Jaywick, Brooklands and Seawick were provided with raised concrete parapets. This increased the height of the walls to 2½ft. above the tide level of the 1953 flood.

To the west of Seawick, the St Osyth marshes were protected by the rebuilding of the earth embankments, which were then faced on their seaward side with concrete blocks. Granite blocks, which had supported the old London Bridge before it was demolished and transported to America, were purchased by the Essex River Authority. Measuring 6ft. x 3ft., they were taken to Holland Haven to be broken up and used in the foundations of the new sea defences.

The crest level of the embankment was raised to 15ft. 9in. This was believed to be sufficient as the marshes would act as a buffer for Jaywick in the event of the embankment being overtopped. Work carried out by the AWA in Jaywick and the surrounding area following the 1978 floods cost £5½ million. In 1979 a wall, higher than the existing one, was built along the 220-yard strip between Fir Way and The Close at a cost of £117,000.

Three hundred and twenty residents were evacuated while these repairs were carried out. Later the authorities began looking to another plan costing £25,000 for the beaches; the Ministry was to be approached to accept the beach recharge plan.

On New Year's Eve 1983, Jaywick was again flooded and people again had to be evacuated. In the same year the Board's engineer, Mr. D. Shipman, said:

> The Tendring peninsula is the most exposed section of the Essex coastline. Apart from cliff sections at Walton, Frinton and Clacton, all the coastal lands are below high water. All this coastal land is protected by sea walls.
>
> Unlike many of the walls elsewhere in Essex, the Tendring walls do not have protective saltings in front of them, but directly face the North Sea and receive the full attack of the waves and storms. The attacks are becoming more and more severe with the continuing loss of protective beaches and foreshores over the years.

When Lord Belstead, the Government's agriculture spokesman in the Lords, was told in 1985 that more than £100 million was needed to repair Essex's sea defences; the sum included £6 million for Jaywick alone. The AWA warned that repair work which had hitherto been held up because of cash restrictions could not be delayed much longer.

The original sea wall, built in 1936, had been patched up in 1978. Mr. Robinson, the principal engineer in charge of the work, said it was no longer adequate.

> The sea is rising at the rate of one foot every hundred years and the beaches are being eroded, leading to the sea walls taking a greater battering. In addition, North Sea surges, which raise the sea level by as much as eight feet above normal, are occurring more often. Building a new wall like the one needed in Jaywick would cost £2,400 a metre—or nearly a million pounds for every 400 metres.

Between 1986 and 1988 the AWA carried out further work at a cost of £11 million to prevent further damage in Jaywick. This work consisted of the construction of four rock-armoured groynes between Jaywick and Martello Bay; the one at Lion Point cost £2 million alone. Huge amounts of sand (some 80,000 cubic metres) were pumped ashore to build up the level of the beaches.

12

After All Those Years

Flushed with Success

After a 40-year battle, the AWA began the installation of main drainage in New Town in 1979. Completed in 1980, it had cost almost £800,000. In their book *Arcadia by The Sea* Dennis Hardy and Colin Ward record Neil Stedman's view on the issue: 'This step was finally taken, because after 40 years the authorities ran out of excuses for ignoring the estate.'

By the 1980s other changes were taking place. Many old businesses had either closed down or changed hands. The charming old farmhouse in Crossways was demolished in 1984. A block of flats had been erected on the site at Donna Drive.

After John Silvers closed a large gift shop on Beach Road, it became the Eldorado Sporting Club and Prize Bingo Hall. This was one of several businesses on the estate Mr. Silvers owned. He bought The Morocco, which passed to his son Paul when he died. Paul sold it in the early 1970s. By 1980 it had changed hands several times until it opened as a late-night disco called The Metro Club, with a Chinese restaurant at the front and a bookmaker to one side.

Ten years later Mr. Thurston bought it for redevelopment, but soon went bankrupt and the building was demolished. Today the site is neglected and full of weeds. Residents would like to see it fenced out of sight.

94   The Eldorado, Beach Road, 1994.

95   Brooklands sea-front in 1935. The building on the left became Pam and Dave's general store in the 1980s.

96   The Morocco Club in 1994. Not a 'site' for sore eyes!

The only launderette on the estate also closed. Located at Rosemary Way, it is now the site of T.S. Glazing, owned and managed by Mr. Tom Studman and his wife Phyllis, both Freehold committee members.

Londoners Pam and Dave, after running a small grocery shop which is now 'Doreen's Diner' in Brooklands Gardens, built a larger shop with living accommodation on the sea-front.

The Health Centre

Following the opening of Golf Green Hall in 1966 a branch surgery was opened and run by partners for just one hour, four days a week. A full-time surgery opened in 1986 in The Close, The Village. This was almost opposite Stedman's second estate office, now a private dwelling.

A new health centre was opened in October 1995, built on the site of the Barn Garage, Jaywick's zoo in 1932. Today Dr. S. Garas looks after 1,900 patients, mostly elderly, some disabled, with an above average number of single-parent families. Dr. Garas was given £15,000 by the health authorities to assist him move to less cramped quarters on Golf Green Road after he had refused a place at the new centre, fearing he might lose his identity.

A chemist's called Kamart & Co. opened in Broom Way, The Village, in 1989. Until then residents had had to travel two miles to Clacton for their prescriptions.

The young people who call Jaywick 'God's waiting room' had to swallow hard when

Mrs. Wyn Pavesley, in her late sixties, blacked up for her 'Jolson Song Days', a song and dance routine, and waltzed off with the top award in the Princes Theatre, Clacton. She was one of the senior citizens who had been performing in the 11th annual Age Concern talent festival.

There are no banks or secondary schools on the estate. Education is provided at Jaywick Primary (Frobisher) School. First built in 1966, it was located at the Tudor Estate. A new one-storey building was erected in 1989 before the old one was demolished. Catering for pupils aged five to 11, who before 1966 had had to

97   The Surgery, The Close, 1994.

98   Residents at a protest meeting in the public hall. Dr. Garas is in the centre, and Councillor Roy Smith is on the far right.

99 Jaywick school was built in the 1960s and rebuilt in the 1980s.

100 Mr. B. Davies, headmaster of Jaywick Primary (Frobisher) School in 1994.

101 Footballers off to beat Cann Hall, 4-1 in 1994.

bus it to Great Clacton, the pretty new building cost £570,000 and can accommodate up to 200 pupils.

Every area has its characters. 'Old Bill' who settled in Jaywick because 'it has a certain magic about it' was one. With silver hair and rosy cheeks, a lover of children, he looked like a garden gnome and was a gifted storyteller; he held them spellbound with tales of Robin Hood, the Pied Piper and other legendary characters.

The old apple tree growing in his back garden was, he insisted, 'Jaywick's Magic Tree'. He promised children that they could have one of four different fruits this tree could produce, if they behaved. Sure enough, in the mornings they found their name written on a piece of paper attached to maybe a ripe strawberry, a cherry, a banana or an orange which was tied on the tree. Because Old Bill's knuckles were twisted with rheumatism, they knew he couldn't tie the fruit on himself and decided it really was a magic tree. Old Bill's friend 'Dead Ted', who only showed signs of life when his shares dropped, kept quiet.

A popular landlady regularly barred punters for life in the evening, only to drive all over the estate the following day to plead for their return. She usually found them supporting another local pub.

Brooklands Community Centre

The lack of play facilities on the estate was recognised by many, and a team of local volunteers, aided by Councillor Fluin, worked hard to get the non-profit making community centre opened in 1993.

Aimed at residents in New Town and located in Brooklands Gardens (next door to the *Mermaid Inn* which is today managed by East Enders Keith and Sharon), the Jaywick Sands Community Hall cost New Tendring £14,000 to buy plus £18,000 for refurbishments. The New Tendring Chairman, Lionel Randall, opened it. Despite all the hard work carried out by the authorities and the associations, there were still many problems that provoked complaints from residents.

In October 1988, Mr. C. Judd, Chairman of the Residents Association, maintained that

as Brooklands promenade had been a public road for more than 20 years the County Council was legally obliged to repair it. Some £18,000 was thought necessary to repair the promenade alone. He called for the unadopted road to be repaired immediately by Essex County Council because Eastern National threatened to pull out of that part of Jaywick unless the road was improved. However, the New Tendring councillors claimed that improving the road would just have the effect of attracting more and more traffic.

All over the country people counted the cost after the hurricane of 14 October 1987. As elsewhere, Jaywick was hit without warning by the worst storm in living memory: roofs were

102 The Ratepayers' membership secretary, Mr. C. Hart, on the right, joins his neighbours in 1978 to help repair their own unadopted road in Gorse Lane, The Village. The materials were a free gift from the local council.

103   Elvina Nursing Home, Meadow Way, built in 1989.

torn off buildings, falling trees blocked roads and 180 caravans, many turned over, were wrecked at the Tower Caravan Park.

Repairs and redevelopments cost the company £300,000, and New Tendring over £345,000. Mr. Matthews told a local reporter: 'It was a catastrophe, everything built up over 23 years was destroyed in one night. If the site had had a land value we would have considered selling.'

The Eldorado News, the estate's free chronicle with a circulation of 2,500, is run by former Beatle Ken Brown. The famous John, Paul and George played with Ken when he formed 'The Quarrymen'—the group played at Liverpool's famous Casbah club in 1958.

Mr. D. Taylor, a partner in the local estate agents Pyrkes, manages the large Sunday market which was once owned by John Bradley & Alan Barry. It opened in March 1977 with 80 stalls, and is located on the site of the old Brooklands car park.

Mr. Taylor has recently purchased The Tivoli and rents it out for storing boats etc.

The Savoy closed and The Playdrome became the Sunspot amusement arcade.

When Butlin's holiday camp closed in 1983, Jaywick was dismayed. Many Jaywickians had worked at the camp over the years, and Sir Billy Butlin had been a very good friend to the whole area.

The Elvina Nursing Home opened in Meadow Way in 1988, on the site of Smith's Amusement Centre opposite *The Sheldrake*. Here the Director Mr. D. Patel and his staff maintain 24-hour care for up to sixty residents.

Crossways hairdresser's, owned and managed by fair-haired Mrs. J. Ferris, is located on the site of the Crossways station. Steve Morris and his wife run a hairdresser's on Broadway.

Glenluce, situated in Flowers Way, is a small residential care home converted from an ordinary bungalow that opened in January 1991. Catering for up to eight mentally-ill residents, its owner Mr. T. Lewis has 20 years' experience in this line of work and takes a personal interest in all his residents.

13

Modern Times

A Diamond Jubilee

Mr. Wright-Clark, Chairman of the association since 1984, led its 1991 Diamond Jubilee celebrations. These included a fête opened by Mr. Neil Stedman. The money raised, £1,105, was spent taking children to Chessington Zoo and giving them a party.

In order to safeguard the assets and security of the association, at its AGM in September 1987, a resolution was passed: 'that no Committee, whether present or in the future, could sell or dispose of, in any way, any property, building, or land without a 75 per cent majority of the members being in favour of any sale'.

A Royal Welcome

Princess Di, wearing a white pleated skirt, a navy-blue jacket and low white heeled shoes bewitched Jaywick on 6 September 1989. She is patron of the Malcolm Sargent Cancer Fund for Children which runs the Malcolm Sargent

104 Residents sea fishing in 1992.

105 The Malcolm Sargent Home for sick children was opened in October 1988. A practical memorial to the musician who was called the 'Ambassador with the baton'.

106 Princess Di, patron of the home gets a royal 'Jaywickian' welcome, September 1989.

House. Located only yards from Foff's Corner, it opened in October 1988 and provides a holiday for up to three families a week. She stayed for two hours. Most local business people support the home, which relies entirely on donations. Warden Eileen Phillips runs the home.

Although most of the estate is smart and well cared for, there are many bungalows boarded up or half derelict. Jaywick did not escape the Poll Tax nor the recession, and many people today are in a sorry financial position.

Jaywick Remembers

January is named from the Roman God Janus who is represented with two faces looking in opposite directions—to the past and to the coming year.

Every year since the 1953 disaster 37 candles have been lit in memory of those who perished. Sunday 29 January 1995 was bitterly cold and it rained heavily. Nevertheless over 100 residents, including survivors and relatives of victims, attended the memorial service held in St Christopher's Church. A plaque bearing the names of the 1953 flood victims was unveiled.

Mrs. Pat Manning, Chairman of New Tendring, unveiled the marble plaque, paid for by donations from Clacton Police, New Tendring (they gave £380), and others. The idea for the plaque was that of Ray and Brenda Olive, the wardens in charge of St Christopher's. Tucking into hot tea and cakes after the service, people got together while journalists and television and radio crews recorded the event.

The dead are part of the story of Jaywick. It is a story which has seen the area develop from a holiday resort into a permanent settlement. It has grown to such an extent that whereas only 100 permanent residents were registered in 1928, by the census of 1981 there were just over 4,000. Tourism still directly and indirectly contributes high levels of expenditure,

107   Memorial service in St Christopher's Church, 1995.

and during the summer the population increases by some 2,000.

Thousands have spent holidays on the estate and many return. Children, including my own niece and nephew, love the memories of the fun they had. 'I sang "Red Sails in the Sunset" every week, for six weeks at a talent contest when I was only ten,' one grandmother recalled between fits of laughter, puzzled because she was always given a prize.

Jaywick has a great deal of old-fashioned charm and a kind heart. A close-knit community, it is always ready to band together to fight for its rights. When Mr. Neil Stedman closed the one remaining Jaywick sales office on Broadway in 1991, it was the end of an era.

Essex is now a fully fledged member of the Assembly of European Regions, and through its office in Brussels the County Council is working with the European Commission to ensure real benefits for the region. It received some £1.5 million in European grants in 1993-4 for a range of training projects, econmic development programmes, social services, libraries and youth projects. Mr. Wright-Clark has applied for grants for new lights and repairs to bridges in New Town.

In November 1995 New Tendring, in partnership with the Freeholders, Essex County Council, the District Council, Essex Police Authority and other organisations, scooped a prize of £1 million for Jaywick. Jaywick had submitted a bid in August 1995 as part of the Local Government Commission's Rural Challenge Competition.

In leading the bid New Tendring aimed to offer the community improved opportunities in employment, education and recreation. Today the community, which was fully involved at all stages of the proposal, can look forward to new investment in projects such as training centres and workshops, together with a new community centre and recreation and play areas. There will also be money to spend on roads, footpaths, public transport and street lighting.

Jaywick has survived against all the odds, and is here to stay. How it will survive in the future—that's another story.

108   A sunny afternoon in Brooklands—Jaywick Sands in the 1930s.

Printed Sources

Banks, I., *Rails to Jaywick Sands* (1988)

Commission for Local Administration in England, 'Investigation 143/H/70' (1980)

Grieve, H., *The Great Tide* (1959)

Hardwick, G., *Paper Clips* (1995)

Hardy, D., and Ward, C., *Arcadia by the Sea* (1994)

Jaywick Sands Freeholders Association Ltd., 'AGM' (1972)

Jacobs, N., *The Sunshine Coast* (1966)

Jacobs, N., *Clacton-on-Sea* (1993)

Morton, E.F., 'A Little Known Essex Miniature Railway', *Essex Countryside* (1976)

National Rivers Authority, 'Battling the Tide' (1992)

Palmer, K., *Setting the Record Straight* (1994)

Porter, J., 'A Chalet by the Sea' (1975)

Stedman, F.C., 'Notes' (1929/32)

Stedman, F.C., 'Property Brochure' (1930s)

Sutcliffe, S., *Martello Towers* (1972)

Tendring District Council, 'Annual Report' (1993/94)

Tendring District Council, 'A Chance in a Lifetime' (1995)

Tendring District Council, 'Minutes & Reports' (1934/58/75/77)

Walker, K., *The History of Clacton* (1966)

Walker, K., 'Jaywick—An Ancient Essex Homestead', *Essex Countryside* (1950)

Walsh, A., 'Strolling around Clacton' (1982)

Index

compiled by Ann Hudson

Page references in bold indicate illustrations.